CONTEMPORARY JEWRY
Volume 8 (Second Annual)

MANUSCRIPT SUBMISSION

Individuals wishing to submit manuscripts for publication consideration are asked to send four (4) copies plus a seif-addressed, stamped postcard for acknowledgment to: Paul Ritterband, Center for Jewish Studies, Box 465/Graduate Center-CUNY, 33 West 42nd Street, New York, New York 10036-8099.

CONTEMPORARY JEWRY
Volume 8 (Second Annual)

Edited by
Arnold Dashefsky

Published for the
Association for the Social Scientific Study of Jewry

Transaction Books
New Brunswick (U.S.A.) and Oxford (U.K.)

ISSN: 0147-1694
ISBN: 0-88738-097-2
Printed in the United States of America

Contents

List of Tables

INTRODUCTION

1

Contemporary Jewry: Review and Overview

Arnold Dashefsky

The recent past of *Contemporary Jewry* may be compared to the experience of the behavior of the people the journal seeks to understand, which is characterized by periodic shifts from penury to prosperity and from famine to feast. I complete my term as editor in what I believe is an upswing period in the sine curve that describes *CJ*'s life history.

Toward a "Content Analysis" of *Contemporary Jewry*

During the recent past (1982 to 1985) of *Contemporary Jewry*'s existence, with which I am most familiar, the volume of submissions has increased. In the two complete years of 1984 and 1985 a total of 30 articles was submitted, averaging nearly 4 (3.8) per three-month quarter (table 1.1). In the beginning period of 1982 and 1983 only 13 articles were submitted, less than three (2.6) per three-month quarter, adjusting for the fact that in 1982 articles were received for only three months.[1] It is important to point out that during this early period there was much discussion as to whether to continue the effort to produce *Contemporary Jewry*. Indeed, with the increase in the pace of submissions, the rate of acceptance has doubled from 15 percent in the earlier period (1982 and 1983) to 30 percent in the more recent period (1984 and 1985). This suggests that both the quantity and quality of submissions have improved dramatically. Fortunately, however, the median turnaround time has remained fairly constant over this period, averaging about six to eight weeks.

But what of the content of the recent issues of *Contemporary Jewry*? Have the subject matter and the data analysis changed? In another source (Dashefsky 1981) I suggested several shifts that might characterize the future trends in the sociological study of American Jewry. They included two hypotheses related to theoretical developments in the study of ethnicity: (1)

1

TABLE 1.1
Article Submissions, Acceptance Rate, and Median Turnaround 1982-1985

Articles	1982[a]	1983	Total 1982-83	1984	1985[b]	Total 1984-85	Total 1982-85
			Years				
Number of submissions	4	9	13[c]	17	13	30[d]	43
Accepted	1	1	2	5	4	9	11
Acceptance rate	25%	11%	15%	29%	31%	30%	26%
Median turnaround time (days)	45	48	48	45	63	52	45

[a] Based on three months.
[b] Two articles arrived during the winter academic recess (1985-86) and were counted in 1985 total.
[c] Quarterly rate = 2.6 (per three months)
[d] Quarterly rate = 3.8 (per three months)

"the results of such a theoretical shift in the sociological study of ethnic relations are likely to produce a literature on the pluralistic responses of American Jews rather than the assimilationist," and (2) "as recognition increases that . . . theoretical approaches . . . can apply to the study of a resurgent ethnic identity more analyses of Jewish identity will be founded on such theories" (Dashefsky 1981, 199-200). In addition, two hypotheses based on methodological innovations in the study of ethnic relations were suggested: (3) "reliance on more complex methodological techniques of analysis and modeling may facilitate the development of a more comprehensive theory of Jewish community or identity," and (4) "future research on American Jewry will reflect a shift to a more comparative focus as foreshadowed by that emphasis in the study of ethnic relations" (Dashefsky 1981, 202). Finally, a fifth hypothesis related to community social policy concerns: (5) "future research will reflect social policy changes associated with budgetary shifts in community priorities" (Dashefsky 1981, 203).

Let me compare the contents of two of the first three journal-formatted issues of *Contemporary Jewry* (i.e. Volume 3, Number 2, Spring/Summer 1977, and Volume 4, Number 2, Spring/Summer 1978)[2] to the two annuals (Volume 7, 1986; and the current Volume 8) with these hypotheses in mind. For purposes of comparison, only the articles and research notes in the latter volumes will be used because they were published on the basis of blind refereed reviews. Therefore, any differences noted more likely reflect changes in the subfield rather than personal editorial decisions.

TABLE 1.2
Characteristics of Articles, 1977-1978 and 1983-1984

	Volumes					
Characteristics of Articles	1977 V3#2	1978 V4#1	Total V3 + V4	1986 V7	Current V8	Total V7 + V8
1. Number of articles (Research Notes)	5	6	11	4	5	9
2. Number of quantitative articles[a]	2	4	6	3	3	6
3. Percentage quantitative articles of total	2/5 (40%)	2/3 (67%)	6/11 (55%)	3/4 (75%)	3/5 (60%)	2/3 (67%)
4. Number of articles in hypothesized directions[b]	1	1	2	3	2	5
5. Percentage articles in hypothesized directions of total	1/5 (20%)	1/6 (17%)	2/11 (18%)	3/4 (75%)	2/5 (40%)	5/9 (56%)

[a] Articles in this category relied on quantitative analysis in the tabular presentation of the data central to the theme of the article.
[b] Articles included in this category reflected at least one of five hypothesized directions: diversification of theoretical approaches focusing on either (1) pluralism or (2) ethnic identity; and/or research innovations using either (3) regression analysis or (4) cross-cultural analysis; and/or (5) community-generated social policy concerns.

Table 1.2 presents a crude attempt to offer a perspective on the changes that have taken place in the content of *Contemporary Jewry* over the past decade. They represent in an approximate way the shift in the nature of research in the field rather than reflect on the individual authors of articles. Thus, the data presented are based on yearly aggregations.

First, line 1 of table 1.2 shows that about the same number of articles (and research notes) were published in the earlier period ($N = 11$) as in the later period ($N = 9$), although a perusal of the current volume reveals a more diverse content. Second, line 3 indicates that the proportion of quantitative articles has increased from slightly more than half in the earlier period (55 percent) to two-thirds in the more recent period. Finally, line 5 reveals that more than half of all articles in the recent period (56 percent) reflected the hypothesized directions: diversification of theoretical approaches focusing on either (1) pluralism or (2) ethnic identity; and/or innovation in research methods using either (3) regression analysis or (4) cross-cultural analysis; and/or (5) community-generated social policy concerns. By contrast, less than a fifth (18 percent) of all articles in the earlier period reflected these concerns. What these data suggest on the basis of this "quick-and-dirty" analysis is that the journal has developed in a more quantitative direction relying on sophisticated methodological analyses. Moreover, community-generated social policy concerns relying on nationwide samples rather than community surveys have become a more important data source for recent articles. To a much lesser extent theoretical approaches reflecting larger emergent interests in the social sciences (e.g. pluralism and ethnic identity) have been slightly more manifest in the current period in comparison to the earlier periods. For the most part these larger theoretical concerns have not been paid much attention by contributors to *Contemporary Jewry*. Perhaps, this observation suggests a future direction.

Overview of Volume 8

The two *articles* featured and two *research notes* presented in this volume are illustrative of these trends. Alan York and Bernard Lazerwitz present a multivariate analysis of the effects of public religious behavior on participation in Jewish voluntary associations based on the National Jewish Population Survey. Jonathan S. Woocher, inspired by a broader theoretical concern about governance in a voluntary polity (from the field of political science), presents a framework for analyzing the degree of democracy in the American Jewish community.

Jay Y. Brodbar-Nemzer, using data from a recent national survey of American Jews, examines sex differences in the attitudes of American Jews toward Israel. Finally, Vivian Klaff presents a comparative analysis of the urban ecology of Jewish populations, using evidence from a variety of metropolitan areas.

The Dialogue and Debate section is a feature initiated in Volume 7. In that volume the focus was on a methodological concern, examining the use of "distinctive Jewish names" (DJN) as a basis for conducting sample surveys in the Jewish community. Volume 8 focuses on a theoretical concern, exploring the linkage between general theoretical understandings of social life and the social scientific study of Jewry. Samuel Klausner addresses the issue in his lead essay, "What Is Conceptually Special about a Sociology of Jewry," and responses are offered by a diverse group of social scientists, namely, Calvin Goldscheider, J. Alan Winter, and Walter P. Zenner.

The Review Essays section seeks to provide the reader with a longer essay than a standard brief review evaluating books of recent importance to the field. Thus, Harold S. Himmelfarb examines the sociology of Talmud study in reviewing William B. Helmreich's *The World of the Yeshiva: An Intimate Portrait of Orthodox Jewry* (1982) and Samuel C. Heilman's *The People of the Book: Drama, Fellowship, and Religion* (1983). Carol Poll, in "American Jewry: Survival or Revival?" reviews two books that treat the larger content of the Jewish community in the United States: Steven M. Cohen's *American Modernity and Jewish Identity* (1983) and Chaim Waxman's *American Jews in Transition* (1983). Last in this section, Steven Bayme writes about one of the most recent and widely reviewed books in the popular press to treat the subject of American Jewry: Charles E. Silberman's *A Certain People: American Jews and Their Lives Today* (1985). Whether readers have had an opportunity previously to read these books or not, they will benefit from the reviews of their colleagues in the field.

In the Appendix Rena Cheskis-Gold and your editor present the continuation of the compendium of citations of abstracts of recent research on contemporary Jewry. Volume 7 presented the citations for 1981 and 1982; the current volume presents those for 1983 and 1984. The actual abstracts (for 1981 and 1982) were for technical reasons published separately for the association at the University of Connecticut. Explorations are ongoing to have the abstracts for succeeding years professionally prepared, published, and distributed to the membership of the association. Volume 8 concludes with notes about the contributors.

Acknowledgments

Returning to the "up-and-down" nature of the fortunes of our journal cited at the outset, I must note that the reason that you, the reader, are able to read these words is due to the dedication and devotion of a number of people to the association and its journal, *Contemporary Jewry*. I extend warm thanks for their assistance and encouragement to J. Alan Winter, Associate Editor; Rena Cheskis-Gold, Assistant Editor; Bernard Lazerwitz, Overseas Editor; Paul Ritterband, Incoming Editor; Egon Mayer, President of ASSJ; Sidney Goldstein, Chair of the Editorial Board; and to all of the other editors and reviewers. To the contributors I offer a sincere thanks for their patience and cooperation in the production of Volume 8. Special thanks are due the staff members of the Center for Judaic Studies and Contemporary Jewish Life of the University of Connecticut, Linda Snyder, Matthew Winiarski and Kimberly Davis, who provided a variety of services in easing the burden of preparing this volume; also to Robert M. Sweeney and Sandra Waldman Dashefsky for their research and editorial assistance; and to Betty Seaver for her copyediting services. In addition, I would like to thank Irving Louis Horowitz, president of Transaction, and Scott B. Bramson, publisher, for their commitment to the continued and speedy publication of *Contemporary Jewry*.

Finally, I want to express my sincere appreciation to all of the members and officers of ASSJ and to the readers of *Contemporary Jewry* for their kind words and continued loyalty to our common effort. It has been my privilege (always!) and pleasure (at times!) to serve the assocation and you as editor of *Contemporary Jewry*. Furthermore, it is my fervent hope that what we have accomplished together is to ensure the continuity, creativity, and contribution of our journal to that body of knowledge we have come to call the Social Scientific Study of Jewry. Thank you, again, for your help.

Notes

1. The editorial offices of *CJ* were moved to the Center for Judaic Studies and Contemporary Jewish Life of the University of Connecticut beginning with the academic year 1982-83. Hence, the articles were submitted for the last three months of 1982.
2. Volume 4, Number 2 (Spring/Summer 1978), was a special thematic issue not including any empirical research articles.

References

Dashefsky, Arnold. 1981. "Theory, Method, and Social Policy in Ethnicity: Developmental Trends in Study of Jews." *Ethnicity* 8:196-205.

ARTICLES

2

Religious Involvement as the Main Gateway to Voluntary Association Activity

Alan York and *Bernard Lazerwitz*

This paper, using National Jewish Population Survey data, seeks to show a general path to voluntary association participation. It finds that public religious behavior (belonging to a synagogue or temple and attendance at services) is associated with participation in Jewish voluntary associations. Thence, a path is indicated either to leadership within the Jewish community or to participation in general voluntary associations. Because this path is similar to one shown in the literature among U.S. Protestants, it is suggested that a general U.S. voluntary association path may be emerging, one that includes both the dominant religious community and minority ethnoreligious groups. The paper also examines the association between participation in voluntary associations and other variables, and finds certain idiosyncrasies in the American Jewish community.

For a considerable number of years sociologists have been trying to clarify the relationships among participation in religious institutions and associations, participation in general community voluntary associations, and a variety of other social characteristics, particularly those associated with social status. For example, Goode (1966) states that of the three variables of private prayer, public church attendance, and activity in religious voluntary associations, only the last is linked with activity in general community voluntary associations. He also thinks it much more likely that it is participation in the general community that leads to participation in religious institutions. Demerath (1965) suggests that high-status Christians have higher involvement with the "churchlike" areas of religion, such as church attendance and parish activity, and low-status Christians are more involved in private religious acts, such as personal prayer or informal religious group activities.

7

Other researchers, such as Litt (1970) and Liebman (1973), assert that religious organization activity serves as a basis for subsequent activity in general voluntary associations. They find this especially true for minority group members. Their conclusions are at odds with the first set of observations.

Goode (1966) and Demerath (1965) picture high social status as the major cause of voluntary association activity and see activity in religious institutions as a manifestation of a prior voluntary activity pattern. Litt (1970) and Liebman (1973) trace activity in general community associations, and subsequent leadership in them, to prior membership and activity in religious or ethnic institutions.

The literature is divided on the subject of voluntary associations and religiosity among American Jews. On the one hand, Lenski (1961) questions if Jewish associational activity bears any connection with religious behavior, and Sklare and Greenblum (1967: 262-63) go further and suggest that Jewish association may be a "secular alternative" for the irreligious, "a means of expressing Jewish identity stripped of the encumbrances of religious interests and sanctions." On the other hand, Liebman (1973:143) sees a strong connection between the two forms of activity and maintains that participation in communal organizations is "a supplement to religious identification." Lazerwitz (1973a), using data from Chicago Jews, looks at the Lenski and Sklare and Greenblum thesis and finds no empirical evidence for their contentions. He suggests that voluntary association participation and religious behavior are, indeed, linked.

In his general activity model, Smith (1980:22) points to significant and positive correlations among all types of discretionary social participation based "on the general accommodation between individual character and culture and social structure." Hence, upward social mobility, which involves filling more social roles, produces an overlap between religious activity and voluntary association activity. Smith views class and religious denomination as ascribed social roles. He places both of them fairly early on a person's casual-time and environmental scales, which produce an individual's discretionary behavior. In Smith's terms, these role linkages may be simultaneous or sequential, and the order of the sequence is not of great importance. However, this view of religion as an ascribed status has been strongly challenged. Yancey et al. (1976) suggest that differences between ethnic and religious groups, and even differences within such groups, are more likely to stem from structural conditions (such as occuption, residential concentration, transportation, and so on) than from ascribed cultural heritage from "the old country."

It is possible, therefore, that one set of circumstances determines voluntary association activity for dominant groups, but this seems unlikely.

Lazerwitz (1973a), Lazerwitz and Harrison (1979), and Harrison and Lazerwitz (1982) bring findings that indicate similar activity patterns hold for Protestants and economically better off minority groups. As a result, one may expect an American national voluntary activity pattern that holds, for the most part, for Protestants and other highly Americanized groups such as Jews and Irish Catholics. This national pattern ought to tie together voluntary association activity, religious participation, and communal leadership. Other minority groups would vary around this national pattern.

As the title of this paper evidences, it is hypothesized that for most adult Americans, prior involvement in a religious institution is the necessary base that leads to voluntary association activity and, for some, community leadership. This assertion will be tested upon the results from a large-scale survey of the U.S. Jewish population that was concerned about activities in synagogue, in Jewish voluntary associations, and in general—not specifically Jewish—voluntary associations.

Data Source

The data presented are from the National Jewish Population Survey (NJPS), a study of the U.S. Jewish population conducted from the early spring of 1970 to the end of 1971 for the Council of Jewish Federations. The sample yielded 5,790 household interviews at a 79 percent response rate. The sample design had to take into account the fact that American Jewry constitutes only a small percentage of the total U.S. population, that a sizable proportion do not live in neighborhoods with high concentrations of Jewish residents, and that many are not listed on readily available communal lists. The final design was a complex, multistage, two-phase, disproportionately stratified cluster sample. The design was guided by a variation of the city directory-block supplement sampling approach described in Lazerwitz (1968) and Kish (1965). Details on the sample, its response characteristics, and generalized sampling errors appear in Lazerwitz (1973b, 1974). When a sampled household was found to contain a Jewish resident, basic information about the family was obtained and, via the Kish (1949) technique, one adult Jewish respondent was then selected for more detailed questioning from among all the Jewish adults in residence. (At this survey phase, there was additional subsampling within just the New York area.) Interviews with 4,305 adult Jewish respondents from the final sampling stage provide the national data reported here.

Variable Definition and Measurement

For reference, we summarize here the variables employed in this report:

1. *Jewish denominational identification and synagogue membership.* Respondents were classified into the Orthodox, Conservative, and Reform categories on the basis of their expressed denominational identifications. Individuals who did not identify with a denomination or said they were "just Jewish" were classified as having no denominational identification. In addition, respondents were classified by whether they were or were not members of a synagogue.
2. *Jewish identification indices.* A set of items indicative of various aspects of religious and ethnic identification were used to create indices of Jewish identification as described in Lazerwitz (1973a, 1978), Lazerwitz and Harrison (1979), and Harrison and Lazerwitz (1982). In brief, these indices are:
   * *Childhood home Jewish background*—an index covering the Jewish aspects of respondent's childhood home and composed of such items as parental religious and Jewish organizational involvement and holiday celebrations.
   * *Jewish education*—the type and amount received during childhood and adolescence.
   * *Religious observance*—an index covering attendance at religious services; and an index covering home religious and ritual observances.
   * *Jewish ideology*—an index on the extent to which being Jewish and retaining Jewish values are believed to be desirable and intrinsically worthwhile.
   * *Jewish primary group involvement*—an index covering the extent to which respondent's dating, courtship behavior, friends, family life, and social life have been confined to Jews.
   * *Jewish socialization of one's children*—degree of respondent's past, present, and anticipated efforts to socialize his or her children into Jewish life.
   * *Concern for world Jewry*—attitudes toward Israel and degree of concern over the fate of Jews in difficult circumstances in the rest of the world.
3. *Jewish organizational involvement.* This was measured by (a) number of organizational memberships, (b) meeting attendance, and (c) activity in and (d) fund-raising for Jewish voluntary associations.
4. *Jewish communal leadership.* This was measured by (a) officership in any Jewish voluntary association, (b) membership in any Jewish "communal" association (those concerned with health, welfare, education, culture, and community relations), (c) membership in organizations classified as "elite" within the community by virtue of their exclusivity, their high status, or their members' high status, and (d) being a "philanthropist"—that is both having a high income *and* giving a large amount of money to charity of any sort.
5. *Activity in general community voluntary associations.* This was measured by (a) number of organizational memberships, (b) meeting atten-

dance, (c) fund-raising for all types of general voluntary associations, and (d) activity in general community health, welfare, education, and civic organizations.
6. *Socioeconomic characteristics.* This covers respondent's education, occupation of the head of the household, total family income for the year prior to the survey, and total amount contributed to charity in the year prior to the survey.[1]
7. *Demographic characteristics.* These cover respondent's sex and age together with
   • *Generation in the United States*—such as respondent foreign-born; both parents foreign-born but respondent born in United States; both parents born in United States, etc.
   • *Family life cycle*—respondents were grouped into ten categories ranging from unmarried respondents, through married couples with young or adolescent children, to couples whose children had left home, to elderly respondents living alone.

The Multivariate Model

The above listing of variables was formed into the complex multivariate model of religioethnic identification given in Lazerwitz (1978) and Harrison and Lazerwitz (1982). This is a recursive model in which the sets of demographic and socioeconomic variables are treated statistically as control blocks so as to permit determining the separate effects of the various religious and ethnic measures.

Next, in obvious order, come those variables associated with childhood, namely, childhood home Jewish background and Jewish education. Then, in time order, comes denominational preference. We assert that most adults have a denominational preference by the time they have reached their twenties. Indeed, the data indicate that among Jews twenty-one to thirty-nine years of age, 83 percent had a denominational preference, although only 41 percent were actually synagogue members.

Next come the two groups of variables involving religious practices both in the home and in the synagogue. Then come four additional measures of Jewish ideology, Jewish primary group involvement, Jewish socialization of children, and concern for world Jewry. The interdisciplinary sequential specificity-time-allocation-life span (ISSTAL) model of Smith (1980) includes *inter alia* the assumptions and content of this model.

Finally, the component parts of the Jewish and general community organizational activity dimensions become the dependent variables. What is of primary interest is the relationships among the demographic, socioeconomic, and Jewish identification indices and the component parts of the Jewish organization activity block, the Jewish leadership block, and the general community activity block.

The component parts of the three activity blocks, Jewish organizational activity, Jewish leadership, and general communal activity, were introduced one by one. This was done by the techniques of path analysis so that an initial activity component, say, number of Jewish or general organizational memberships, went from being an initial dependent variable to being an intervening variable when the next activity component entered the regression equation as a dependent variable.

Data Analysis

The model data were analyzed by the OSIRIS multivariate analysis program (Rattenbury and Van Eck, 1973). Its three basic components, called automatic interaction detection (AID), multiple classification analysis (MCA), and multivariate nominal scale analysis (MNA), were used to create regression equations.

Both MCA and MNA are variations of dummy variable multiple regression procedures. They assume an additive model but need no assumption of linearity. The chief advantage of these programs is that the predictor variables can be ordinal or nominal. Although MCA requires an interval or pseudointerval scale for dependent variables, MNA is able to work with nominal or ordinal dependent variables. MCA was used for those dependent variables on a nearly interval scale (number of Jewish and general organization memberships); the remaining dependent variables, all of which are nominal, were analyzed using MNA. Both the MCA and MNA programs give beta measures that depict the ability of a predictor variable to explain changes in the dependent variable after adjusting for the effects of all the other predictor variables.

MCA and MNA assume that there are no interactions among the variables, and so the AID program was used first to check that. No meaningful interactions were found, and it may be assumed that any interactions that were not detected by the AID analysis have very limited impacts, if any at all, and may be ignored.

Findings

Following the statistical criteria of previous work with these models of Jewish identification, beta coefficients of .09(− .09) or less are considered weak values. Beta coefficients from .10(− .10) to .19(− .19) are considered of moderate strength; beta coefficients of .20(− .20) or more are regarded as strong values (see Lazerwitz [1978] or Harrison and Lazerwitz [1982] for similar usage of betas).[2]

Table 2.1 introduces the model for participation in Jewish voluntary associations. The predictor variables appear in the horizontal array (columns); the various dependent variables appear in the vertical array (rows). The figures given in the table are beta coefficients derived from MCA and MNA calculations. The MCA or MNA squared multiple correlation term appears in the final data column. Then, each table row represents the beta coefficients of one dummy variable multiple regression equation with the indicated dependent variable, predictor variables, and resultant multiple correlations. For example, the first equation of table 2.1 has membership in Jewish voluntary associations as the dependent variable. The beta coefficient between Jewish association membership and sex is $-.14$; between Jewish association membership and world Jewry concern, .09. That equation's squared multiple correlation coefficient is .37. The remainder of table 2.1 and all of tables 2.2 and 2.3 can be read in the same way.

Observing the betas of table 2.1, one sees that women join Jewish organizations more than men. However, once people are in such organizations, sex differences count for little. Life cycle influences attendance at meetings, with those families having schoolchildren being the ones with good attendance records. Again, respondents coming from more Jewishly identified childhood homes are more likely to join Jewish associations. After they have joined, this index no longer has an impact. There is also a tendency for those from homes where parents were involved in Jewish organizations to be more involved in such organizations.

Jewish education shows its moderate influence in greater attendance at meetings. A socioeconomic variable with a moderate impact is occupation of head. Those belonging to families in which the head has a higher-status occupation are more likely to be active and to attend meetings.

What really counts is not just having money but being willing to give it. Note that our charity variable has a strong association with joining Jewish voluntary associations and a consistently moderate influence upon both attendance and fund-raising activities. Finally, note that first synagogue membership and, then, attendance at religious services are clearly influential in both joining associations and being active in them. Unlike charity, however, neither of these two is influential upon fund-raising.

Now, turn to table 2.2, which continues the equations of table 1. The dependent variables are those of Jewish voluntary leadership. Following a path analysis approach, the table places the dependent variables of table 2.1, participation in Jewish voluntary associations, as the final group of predictor variables. The same patterns observed in the previous table appear here. Sex shows a limited specific impact again, with membership in the communal organizations being predominantly female. Higher levels of education and occupation are associated with philanthropy. Charity contri-

TABLE 2.1
MCA and MNA Beta and Multiple Correlation Values for the Jewish Associational Participation Model, NJPS, 1971 (N = 4,305)

Predictor Variables	Bio-Social			Jewish Background				Socioeconomic					Religious Practice						
Dependent Variables	Sex	Gen in U.S.	Life Cycle	Home	Educ.	Father's Orgs.	Mother's Orgs.	Inc.	Charity	Educ.	Occ.	Denom.	Sabbath Obs.	Passover Obs.	Chanuka Obs.	Kashrut Obs.	Yom K. Obs.	Syn. Att. Obs.	Syn. Memb.
J. assn. participation																			
Membership	−.14	.08	.09	.11	.06	.06	.10	.07	.31	.08	.08	−.05	.03	.02	.02	.01	.01	.20	.15
Attendance																			
High	−.08	.09	.10	.03	.14	.11	.10	−.13	.14	.02	.09	.02	.03	.05	.03	.05	.01	.13	.10
Poor	−.02	−.04	.12	.07	.03	−.10	.05	.09	.09	.09	.06	−.05	.11	.00	.04	.03	.01	−.12	−.03
Non	−.05	.05	.10	.03	−.10	−.05	.03	.09	.10	.05	.10	.06	.05	.04	.00	.06	.01	.04	.12
Nonmember	.11	.06	.14	−.09	−.03	−.04	.11	−.10	−.19	.09	.10	.05	.03	.01	.01	.03	.01	−.16	−.13
Activity																			
High	−.04	.07	.09	.06	.08	.04	.09	.07	.19	.08	.11	.05	.00	.00	.02	.00	.02	.17	.04
Moderate	.03	.07	.06	.08	.09	.06	−.13	.09	−.14	−.10	.15	−.07	.01	.02	.01	.02	.01	.15	.01
None	.00	−.07	.08	.03	−.13	−.07	.05	−.07	−.13	.05	.15	.02	.02	.02	.02	.02	.02	−.24	−.03
Fundraising	−.02	.03	.07	.06	.04	.05	.07	.04	.12	.03	.06	.07	.02	.01	.00	.03	.00	.05	.05

TABLE 2.1 (continued)

Predictor Variables	Jewish Identification				Jewish Organization Participation				Jewish Leadership			Squared Mult. Corr.
Dependent Variables	Ideol.	Primary Group Involve.	Social. of Children	World Jewry	Member-ship	Attend-ance	Activ-ity	Fund-raising	Officer	Communal Orgs.	Elite Orgs.	
J. assn. *participation*												
Membership	.05	.08	.03	.09								.37
Attendance												
High	.07	.10	−.05	.04	—							.20
Poor	.06	.07	.00	.08	—							.20
Non	.01	.00	.05	.07	—							.20
Nonmember	.05	−.12	−.02	−.06	—							.20
Activity												
High	.07	.05	.03	.04	—	—						.20
Moderate	.04	.11	.02	.09	—	—						.20
None	.09	−.12	.03	−.09	—	—						.20
Fundraising	.04	.03	.05	.04	.29	.24	.35					.27

Note: Minus sign = women more than men; foreign-born more than third generation; Reform more than Orthodox; low category more than high category.

TABLE 2.2
MNA Beta and Multiple Correlation Values for the Communal Leadership Model, NJPS, 1971 (N = 4,305)

Predictor Variables	Bio-Social			Jewish Background				Socioeconomic					Religious Practice						
	Sex	Gen in U.S.	Life Cycle	Home	Educ.	Father's Orgs.	Mother's Orgs.	Inc.	Charity	Educ.	Occ.	Denom.	Sabbath Obs.	Passover Obs.	Chanuka Obs.	Kashrut Obs.	Yom K. Obs.	Syn. Att.	Syn. Memb.
Dependent Variables																			
Jewish assoc. officers	-.01	04	.05	.04	.01	.02	.02	.03	.06	.02	.07	.02	.02	.02	.01	.00	.01	.02	.00
Jewish community organization members	-.18	.03	.08	.10	.05	.02	.08	.09	.14	.09	.08	-.06	.05	.00	.00	.09	.01	.11	.01
Jewish elite organization members	.02	.01	.06	.04	.04	.02	.03	.05	.18	.07	.15	-.08	.02	.03	.04	-.05	.01	.10	.05
Philanthropists	.01	.05	.11	-.02	.03	.03	.03	—	.11	.11	.16	-.05	.00	.02	.04	-.04	.03	.07	.03

TABLE 2.2 (continued)

Predictor Variables / Dependent Variables	Jewish Identification				Jewish Organization Participation				Jewish Leadership			Squared Mult. Corr.
	Ideol.	Primary Group Involve.	Social. of Children	World Jewry	Member-ship	Attend-ance	Activ-ity	Fund-raising	Officer	Communal Orgs.	Elite Orgs.	
Jewish assoc. officers	.03	.01	.02	.01	.07	.13	.49	.09				.38
Jewish community organization members	.08	.04	.02	.08	—	—	—	.13	.11			.24
Jewish elite organization members	.02	.04	-.03	.05	—	—	—	.07	.08	—		.17
Philanthropists	.04	.00	-.05	.06	.36	.24	.05	.08	.01	.01	.12	.20

Note: Minus sign = women more than men; foreign-born more than third generation; Reform more than Orthodox; low category more than high category.

TABLE 2.3
MCA and MNA Beta and Multiple Correlation Values for the General Associational Participation Model, NJPS, 1971 (N = 4,305)

Predictor Variables	Bio-Social			Jewish Background				Socioeconomic					Religious Practice						
Dependent Variables	Sex	Gen in U.S.	Life Cycle	Home	Educ.	Father's Orgs.	Mother's Orgs.	Inc.	Charity	Educ.	Occ.	Denom.	Sabbath Obs.	Passover Obs.	Chanuka Obs.	Kashrut Obs.	Yom K. Obs.	Syn. Att.	Syn. Memb.
General assn. participation																			
Membership	.12	.13	.11	.04	.07	.05	.04	.03	.16	.07	.21	−.09	.06	.01	.03	−.04	−.04	.07	.05
Attendance																			
High	−.01	.12	.14	−.08	−.04	.07	.13	.02	.06	.05	.09	.05	−.04	.03	.04	.00	.05	.04	.01
Poor	.04	.09	.15	−.16	−.08	.05	.05	.05	.06	.09	.10	−.06	−.03	.01	.00	.03	.00	.06	.04
Non	.12	.06	.16	.08	.07	.10	.04	.12	.03	.08	.09	.03	.05	−.05	.05	.00	−.05	.03	.00
Nonmember	−.10	.11	.15	.12	.09	.06	−.13	−.06	−.06	−.12	.16	.06	.01	.04	−.06	.03	.00	.04	−.04
Fundraising	−.12	.06	.11	.09	.07	.05	.06	.03	.06	.08	.08	.03	.02	.05	.01	−.07	.01	.03	.00
Communal organization members	−.08	.16	.17	.12	−.06	−.08	.11	.09	.02	.15	.05	−.07	.04	.03	.02	−.01	−.04	.13	.01

TABLE 2.3 (continued)

Predictor Variables	Jewish Identification				Jewish Organization Participation				Jewish Leadership			Squared Mult. Corr.
Dependent Variables	Ideol.	Primary Group Involve.	Social. of Children	World Jewry	Member-ship	Attend-ance	Activ-ity	Fund-raising	Officer	Communal Orgs.	Elite Orgs.	
General assn. participation												
Membership	.02	−.05	−.01	.02	.14	.25	.04	.14				.30
Attendance												
High	−.02	−.06	−.07	−.05	.46	.41	.12	.00	—			.21
Poor	−.13	.14	.09	.03	.09	.14	.06	.08	—			.21
Non	.02	.04	.03	.04	−.49	.67	−.10	.01	—			.21
Nonmember	.08	.08	.04	.02	−.07	.10	−.05	−.06	—			.21
Fundraising	.06	.03	−.02	.03	.06	.08	.07	.32	.04	.20		.27
Communal organization members	.03	.06	−.02	.04	.20	.29	.06	.00	—	—	.12	.26

Note: Minus sign = women more than men; foreign-born more than third generation; Reform more than Orthodox; low category more than high category.

butions and synagogue attendance are associated with membership in both the communal and the elite Jewish voluntary associations. Finally, as would be expected, officers are those who are active in Jewish associations, and both membership and activity are strongly associated with philanthropy.

Finally, table 2.3 maintains the same predictor model but introduces as the dependent variables those measuring activity in general voluntary associations. However, note that the dependent variables of table 2.2 (Jewish communal leadership) are not predictor variables in table 2.3. Although it had been anticipated that Jewish leadership would have an effect on participation in general associations, the data showed otherwise. Thus, when the four Jewish leadership variables of table 2.2 were used as predictors in an MCA run in which the dependent variable was a composite index of general organizational activity, the beta values were respectively .02, $-.01$, .01, and .03. Therefore, it is possible to drop the weak Jewish leadership variables from table 2.3.

As one would expect from previous research, table 2.3 shows that men, those with more generations in the United States and those with older children, are more likely to join general (non-Jewish) voluntary associations, to become active in them, and to be members of the so-called communal organizations. Beyond these basic variables, the only intervening variables consistently associated with the various measures of general associational participation are those measuring activity in Jewish voluntary associations.

The squared multiple regression coefficients are .25 or above for Jewish association membership and fund-raising (table 2.1), being an officer in a Jewish association (table 2.2), and, in table 2.3, membership in general community voluntary associations, membership in a general communal organization, and fund-raising for general community organizations.

What do these three complex tables tell us? Jewish background, denomination, home religious practices, and Jewish identification predictors have very little effect on Jewish voluntary association participation. Sex has an effect on affiliation, and life cycle on attendance. Among the socioeconomic predictors, charity contribution shows consistently moderate to strong effects and occupation has a moderate effect on activity. Synagogue membership and, to a greater extent, religious service attendance both have moderate impacts on participation in Jewish associations.

Leadership in the Jewish community is strongly associated with participation in Jewish associations. The predictors involving demography, Jewish background, denomination, home religious practices, and Jewish identification seldom reach even moderate effects.

Participation in general community associations is best associated with activity in Jewish voluntary associations. On the whole, socioeconomic variables have little impact; the demographic factors, which are of little importance in the previous tables, are more prominent in table 2.3. The predictors of Jewish background, religious practice (home and public), and Jewish identification have virtually no effect on the general community dependent variables.

Conclusions

Before returning to the major thesis of this article, the connection between religious involvement and voluntary activity, let us consider the effects of socioeconomic status and demographic variables. What the data of the National Jewish Population Survey seem to show is that socioeconomic status *qua* status is no longer (if it ever was) of importance for participation and leadership within the Jewish community. It is the translation of that status into charity contributions that is important within the American Jewish community. Activity in Jewish associations and leadership within the community require the American Jew to give, not just to have.[3]

It may be argued that socioeconomic status in general, and wealth in particular, have declined in importance in the American Jewish community as it has moved toward greater homogeneity. Laumann and Segal (1971), who also find a lack of association between socioeconomic status and associational participation, maintain that for over two generations and more, the Jews of the United States have enjoyed a stability of their high achieved status, have become more homogeneous, and so are less differentiated by factors of socioeconomic status. Glazer (1977) concludes that the leadership of American Jews today is less dependent on wealth, partly owing to the homogeneity of the community and the relatively large number of those who are wealthy enough to undertake communal leadership, and partly because of the increasing influence of the professional workers, whose importance in the large organizations outweighs that of the titular leaders.[4]

This research shows that the typical American Jewish communal leader is not considerably more wealthy nor of a higher occupational status than other American Jews. He or she is more generous to Jewish and other charities.

Although occupation and charity have a moderate impact on general associational membership, and education has a moderate impact on membership in general communal organizations, on the whole the measures of socioeconomic status have little force in the general associational participation equations. On the other hand, the demographic factors, particularly family life cycle but also sex and United States generation, have a fairly consistent, moderate effect on the four measures of general associational participation. The conclusion is that young to middle-aged parents, whose children are still at home, are the American Jews who join and participate in general associations.

Although American Jews are becoming increasingly homogeneous socioeconomically, demographic heterogeneity must remain. Sklare and Greenblum (1967) have drawn a picture of the child-orientation of the associations of American Jews. This picture is not supported by the data for Jewish associational participation, but it does seem to apply to participation in general associations. The two types of general associations most frequently joined by American Jews are professional and trade organizations (16 percent of the sample are members of at least one) and parentteacher associations (10 percent of the respondents). The former type serves the occupational role; the latter, and other associations of its type, serves the family role. The family role is, therefore, an important element in becoming a member of, and being active in, general associations.

The findings of the National Jewish Population Survey support the thesis of Liebman (1973) and Lazerwitz (1973a), not that of Lenski and Sklare and Greenblum (1967). Voluntary associations and public religious behavior supplement and complement each other, and do not act as alternatives. Those who belong to a synagogue, and attend it with even moderate regularity, are much more likely to become involved in Jewish voluntary associations than those who are not affiliated with a synagogue nor attend one with some regularity.

It may be argued that church attendance is part of the U.S. middle-class norm, and so the Jew who attends voluntary associations, particularly general associations, is more likely to attend synagogue. However, this sequence implies prior attendance at general voluntary associations and there meeting the norm of church attendance of the American Christians who are one's fellow members. The data do not support this argument, for they show no impact of synagogue attendance on general association membership, while its impact on Jewish association membership is marked. Our conclusion is that American Jews first identify with a denomination, then affiliate with a synagogue and attend its services. Then, through informal and formal social activities in and around that synagogue, many become more involved in Jewish activities and, therefore, in Jewish voluntary associations. Jewish associationalism is, indeed, a natural continuation of activity in the synagogue, as is shown historically by Levitats (1959), and the connection has not been broken in the United States of the twentieth century.

The models draw a path of participation from the synagogue to the Jewish association, and thence either onward into deeper responsibility within the Jewish community or into participation in voluntary associations in the general (non-Jewish) community. They strengthen the case for the mobilization or socialization effect of participation, for the effect appears to be general and not connected with personal attitudes or characteristics. Rogers et al. (1975) find that the mobilization effect holds more strongly among those of higher socioeconomic status, and this appears to be the case with the American Jewish community. The synagogue socializes American Jews into further voluntary activity, and the Jewish voluntary association socializes them into participation in general voluntary associations. As Rogers et al. (1975) put it, organizational involvement leads to personal skills and satisfaction, and these, in turn, lead to further and other types of participation.

The literature on the functions of voluntary associations sees them as, *inter alia*, instruments of integration into society and as channels of communication (Litwak, 1961; Smith, 1966; Young and Larson, 1965). It seems that the American Jewish voluntary association network is indeed fulfilling these functions in its socialization of American Jews to take part in similar activities in the wider community. Thus, American Jewish organizations are not a means of cultural isolation for American Jews but a socializing influence for them to take a greater part in their own community and in U.S. society in general.

The parallels noted above between American Jews and Protestants support an even broader conclusion. The writings of Demerath (1965), Stark (1966), and others have put forward a path to voluntary associations for American Protestants: from "churchlike" public religious behavior to voluntary associations, within their religious community and without.[5] The National Jewish Population Survey data show that the path to voluntary association is similar for American Jews. This, therefore, appears to be a U.S. voluntary association path, linked specifically neither with the dominant U.S. religious community nor with a minority religioethnic group. For the majority of U.S. voluntary association activists, religious involvement is the main gateway to further activity.

Notes

The authors thank the council of Jewish Federations and Welfare Funds for permission to use these data from the survey it commissioned.

1. The data on income and charity contribution could have been seriously impaired by the relatively high number of those who refused to answer these questions or were unable to do so. Almost a fifth of the respondents answered either or both of these questions in one of these ways, though almost all of them answered all of these questions. In order not to lose these respondents, it was decided to include "don't know" and refusals in the moderate category of income and charity. By the law of averages, many of them were indeed moderate earners and charity donors. Moreover, OSIRIS impacts come mainly from the difference between highest and lowest categories, and so the moderate category, even if it is overrepresented, should not affect the results too drastically. The bias caused by this treatment would tend to moderate the effects of both variables.
2. The reader unfamiliar with OSIRIS may be surprised not to find any significant testing. The reasons for this are found in detail in Harrison and Lazerwitz (1982: 363-64), but, in brief, they stem from the complex, multistage, clustered sample on the one hand (see Lazerwitz [1974] on this) and the use of MNA on the other (see Kish and Frankel [1970] on the difficulties involved here). Thus, this article relies upon the presence of consistent data patterns, and the authors consider that with such a large N , it is unlikely that these patterns result from chance variations.
3. There are exceptions to this pattern. Sutker (1950) describes the case of Jewish "aristocrats" in Atlanta, descendants of the German-speaking immigrants who came in the mid-nineteenth century, who retained their leadership positions owing to their ascribed status. Although the descendants of the Eastern European immigrants were wealthier and more generous to charity, they lacked prestige in the Jewish and general community, and were still considered newcomers in the mid-twentieth century. Elazar (1976: 277-79) suggests that academics are another exception, but points out that few are active in Jewish associations.
4. It must be emphasized, however, that the data in this research come from a large, representative sample of American Jewry, and so the leaders described and discussed here include the whole spectrum of American Jewish leadership, from the secretary of a small lodge to the president of a national organization. At best, given sampling considerations, few of the national leaders entered the sample, and it would be unjustified to draw conclusions from the survey data about the very small numbers who make up the members of the Conference of Presidents of major Jewish organizations.
5. Greeley (1976), in the concluding remarks to his analysis of the comparative status achievements of U.S. ethnic and denominational groups, suggests that the high achievements of the Catholic ethnic groups may be rooted in their homogeneous primary groups. May this not be another example of the phenomenon shown among American Jews?

References

Demerath, N.J., III. 1965. *Social Class in American Protestantism*. Chicago. Rand McNally.
Elazar, Daniel J. 1976. *Community and Polity*. Philadelphia: Jewish Publication Society.
Glazer, Nathan. 1977. "American Jewish Leadership." *Contemporary Jewry* 3:3-16.
Goode, Erich. 1966. "Social Class and Social Participation." *American Journal of Sociology* 72:102-11.

Greeley, Andrew M. 1976. *Ethnicity, Denomination and Inequality.* Sage Research Papers in the Social Sciences, vol. 4, series no. 90-029 (Studies in Religion and Ethnicity). Beverly Hills: Sage Publications.

Harrison, Michael, and Bernard Lazerwitz. 1982. "Do Denominations Matter?" *American Journal of Sociology* 88: 356-77.

Kish, Leslie. 1949. "A Procedure for Objective Respondent Selection within the Household." *Journal of the American Statistical Association* 44:380-87.

———. 1965. *Survey Sampling.* New York: Wiley.

Kish, Leslie, and Martin Frankel. 1970. "Balanced Repeated Replications for Analytical Statistics." *Journal of the American Statistical Association* 65: 1071-94.

Laumann, Edward O., and David R. Segal. 1971. "Status Inconsistency and Ethnoreligious Group Membership as Determinants of Social Participation and Political Attitudes." *American Journal of Sociology* 77:36-61.

Lazerwitz, Bernard. 1968. "Sampling Theory and Procedures." In *Methodology in Social Research*, ed. Hubert M. and Ann B. Blalock, pp. 278-328. New York: McGraw-Hill.

———. 1973a. "Religious Identification and Its Ethnic Correlates." *Social Forces* 52:204-20.

———. 1973b. *The Sample Design of the National Jewish Population Survey.* New York: Council of Jewish Federations.

———. 1974. *Sampling Errors and Statistical Inference for the National Jewish Population Survey.* New York: Council of Jewish Federations.

———. 1978. "An Approach to the Components and Consequences of Jewish Identification." *Contemporary Jewry* 4:3-8.

Lazerwitz, Bernard, and Michael Harrison. 1979. "American Jewish Denominations: A Social and Religious Profile." *American Sociological Review* 44:656-66.

Lenski, Gerhard. 1961. *The Religious Factor.* Garden City, N.Y.: Doubleday.

Levitats, Isaac. 1959. "The Jewish Association in America." In *Essays on Jewish Life and Thought*, ed. Joseph L. Blau et al. New York: Columbia University Press.

Liebman, Charles S. 1973. "American Jewry: Identity and Affiliation." In *The Future of the Jewish Community in America*, ed. David Sidorsky. New York: American Jewish Committee.

Litt, Edgar. 1970. *Beyond Pluralism: Ethnic Politics in America.* Glenview, Ill.: Scott, Foresman.

Litwak, Eugene. 1961. "Voluntary Associations and Neighborhood Cohesion." *American Sociological Review* 25:258-71.

Rattenbury, Judith, and Neal Van Eck. 1973. *OSIRIS: Architecture and Design.* Ann Arbor: Institute for Social Research, University of Michigan.

Reddy, Richard R. 1980. "Individual Philanthropy and Giving Behavior." In *Participation in Social and Political Activities*, ed. David Horton Smith, Jacqueline Macaulay, and associates, pp. 370-99. San Francisco: Jossey-Bass.

Rogers, David L., Gordon L. Bultena, and Ken H. Barb. 1975. "Voluntary Association Membership and Political Participation." *Sociological Quarterly* 16:305-18.

Sanua, Victor D. 1964. "Patterns of Identification with the Jewish Community in the United States of America." *Jewish Journal of Sociology* 6:190-212.

Sklare, Marshall, and Joseph Greenblum. 1967. *Jewish Identity on the Suburban Frontier.* New York: Basic Books.

Sklare, Marshall, and Mark Vosk. 1957. *The Riverton Study.* New York: American Jewish Committee.
Smith, David Horton. 1966. "The Importance of Formal Voluntary Organizations for Society." *Sociology and Social Research* 50: 483-92.
_____. 1980. "Methods of Inquiry and Theoretical Perspectives"; "Determinants of Individuals' Discretionary Use of Time"; "General Activity Model." In *Participation in Social and Political Activities*, ed. David Horton Smith, Jacqueline Macauley, and associates, pp. 8-33; 34-75; 461-530. San Francisco: Jossey-Bass.
Stark, Rodney. 1966. *The Economics of Piety.* Berkeley: University of California Survey Research Center.
Sutker, Solomon. 1950. "The Jews of Atlanta." PH.D. diss., University of North Carolina, Chapel Hill.
Yaffe, James. 1968. *The American Jews.* New York: Random House.
Yancey, William L., Eugene P. Ericksen, and Richard N. Juliani. 1976. "Emergent Ethnicity: A Review and Reformulation." *American Sociological Review* 41: 391-403.
Young, Ruth C., and Olaf F. Larson. 1965. "The Contribution of Voluntary Organizations to Community Structure." *American Journal of Sociology* 71: 178-86.

3

The Democratization of the American Jewish Polity

Jonathan S. Woocher

For almost as long as there has been an organized Jewish community in North America, there has been debate about the extent to which that community is, can, and should be governed democratically. Such discussion has often been polemical rather than analytical. As applied to Jewish communal life, "democracy" can be operationalized in terms of seven political processes: (1) access; (2) participation; (3) representation; (4) debate; (5) accountability; (6) communication; and (7) political development. In general, the Jewish community is governed by a trusteeship rather than by formally representative institutions. The system, however, is not designed to be exclusionary, and leaders are broadly representative in their attitudes of the Jewish populace as a whole. Recent developments have made Jewish communal governance somewhat more democratic by bringing in new leadership elements and broadening the agenda of public action. Nevertheless, many problem areas remain, and there is some doubt about whether the Jewish community ever can or should be as democratic as its critics urge.

Democracy and Jewish Communal Governance

In November 1969 a young Jewish graduate student, Hillel Levine, stood before several thousand delegates to the General Assembly of the Council of Jewish Federations and delivered a ringing indictment of the Jewish communal establishment. Jewish federations, the dominant institutions in the Jewish power structure in the United States, were, he charged, out of touch with the real needs of Jewish life in the United States.

> Federations must seek not only the financial support, but also the guidance and leadership of a broader constituency from the American Jewish com-

27

munity. It can no longer be run by a few generous men or the patrons of particular projects whose concerns do not transcend their project. Rabbis, people involved in Jewish education, Jewish scholars, students, and concerned Jews should participate on all levels of decision making and allocations [Levine 1973, 192-93].

Levine's call for broadened participation in federation decision making reflected a common perception among critics of Jewish communal organization during that turbulent period of the late 1960s. Writing during that same year, a veteran Jewish communal leader and critic, Judah Shapiro, put the matter even more boldly:

In a comparison with industry, the Jewish Federations come out a poor second, even with respect to the superficial aspects of democratic procedures. . . . In Jewish Federations there is no election in which the shareholders have voice with respect to the selection of leadership, the approval of policy, or the choice of alternatives. There is not even a poll of sentiment with respect to actions taken. This means, in fact, that there is no accountability of the leadership to the contributors, to the Federation's constituency [Shapiro 1973, 203-4].

The judgment that U.S. Jewish Federations are un- (if not actually anti-) democratic has not been limited to a handful of communal activists. Marc Raphael has been no less forceful in his evaluations:

Most Federations make little or no pretense of democracy, viewing it as an impediment to efficient operation. . . . "Democratic" decision-making— where as broad as possible a basis of participation is involved in the process (small and large contributors equally)—remains what "ought" to be, nowhere what "is" [Raphael 1979, 153, 158].

These contemporary critiques have ample antecedents in the history of American Jewish communal life. For almost as long as there has been an American Jewish community, there has been discussion and debate over its organization and governance. Yet, like the statements cited above, most of that discussion has been polemical rather than analytic. "Democracy" has been a slogan in the mouths of political contestants, but a host of conceptual and empirical issues have gone largely unexplored. What might *democracy* mean when applied to the Jewish community? To what extent does the governance of the community—and especially of the Jewish federations, its contemporary "framing institutions" (Elazar 1982, 12-13)—approach a democratic ideal? What changes in the patterns and processes of communal governance have taken place in recent years, and have they enhanced the democratic character of federations? Is democracy, in fact, an appropriate model for the governance of the Jewish polity?[1]

These issues are worth exploring for their intrinsic interest and because they constitute a potentially illuminating test case for the applicability of political science concepts and approaches to the study of American Jewish life. By now, the identification of the American Jewish community as (among other things) a voluntary polity has become commonplace. But systematic political research on the Jewish community—how it operates as a polity—and attempts to link that research to broader political science theory are still relatively uncommon. The issue of democratization—in part precisely because it has been one of the perennial "slogans" of American Jewish political rhetoric—provides an excellent opportunity to see whether social science can, in fact, help to advance what has often been a sterile debate. This paper is intended to be a beginning in that endeavor.

Toward an Operational Concept of Democracy

The first obstacle we face in exploring the state of democracy in Jewish communal governance and trends toward enhanced or lessened democracy in recent years is the difficulty of defining *democracy* itself. As Robert Dahl notes at the outset of his *Preface to Democratic Theory* (1956) political thought from Aristotle onward provides a plethora of democratic theories that are by no means agreed on either the goals or the characteristics of a democratic political system. What becomes clear in examining both the theories and the experience of what are by common consent democracies is that simple definitions equating *democracy* with "popular sovereignty," "majority rule," or "political equality" are inadequate. Indeed, some contemporary efforts to typologize systems of political control avoid the term altogether, preferring, for example, to categorize regimes as "autocratic," "oligarchic," or "polyarchic" (with appropriate subcategories) (cf. Elazar 1970).

Perhaps equally as vexing is the problem of distinguishing "formal" from "substantive" democracy. Typically, characterizations of *democracy* begin with formal characteristics: election of officeholders, decision making by majority vote, public meetings at which issues are discussed. By these criteria, federations and nearly every other American Jewish organization, are undeniably democratic. But the existence of formal democracy, though obviously critical as the infrastructure without which a more substantive, operational democracy could not exist, is obviously not what concerns the critics of the Jewish communal system. The issue they raise is one of distribution of real power. Do elections and votes in fact decide anything, or are they merely vehicles for ratifying decisions already arrived at by other means?

We would, therefore, suggest an alternative approach to operationalizing the concept of democracy for use in the Jewish organizational context. We will focus on a set of political conditions and processes that are often associated with democratic governance but that can be examined without getting trapped in the definitional bog that surrounds the term itself. To answer adequately the questions we have posed about the state of democracy in the American Jewish polity—and especially in seeking to assess recent trends—we should consider seven different (albeit often related) aspects of the communal political process:

1. *Access*—Who is heard in the political process? What channels are available for reaching decision-making centers? What are the modes for making one's views and concerns known?
2. *Participation*—Who is actually involved in decision making, for what range of issues, and in what ways?
3. *Representation*—To what extent do decision makers represent the members of the community? How are various interests, ideologies, and subcommunities represented? What type of representation does the system embody?
4. *Debate*—Are policy alternatives considered and openly discussed by decision makers?
5. *Accountability*—To whom or what are decision makers accountable in their actions?
6. *Communication*—How are members of the community made aware of decisions? What mechanisms exist for providing feedback on the effectiveness of policies to decision makers?
7. *Political development*—To what extent does the system build political community? How effective is it in the tasks of political socialization, recruitment, and citizenship education?

Though we cannot hope to be exhaustive in this brief essay, these categories provide us with both a more manageable and meaningful set of questions to pose of the data available, and a research agenda for more detailed future exploration.

Trusteeship Governance

What, then, can be said about the state of democracy in the American Jewish polity? The truth, it would seem, probably lies somewhere between the dismal picture painted by critics and the relatively sanguine reassurances offered by some defenders of the current system. Indeed, as one begins to examine the evidence, one is struck by the extent to which it can be used to support the central claims of both parties in the debate. This reflects in part the nature of the evidence itself. There have, as we noted above, been very few systematic empirical studies of Jewish communal governance in North America. By and large, critics, defenders of the system, and purportedly objective observers all cite anecdotal and impressionistic evidence. Because we are concerned with decision making, inferences can occasionally be drawn from the substance of the decisions themselves about the process through which they were arrived at. But in general, lacking detailed case materials, community studies, and policy research, we must rely on perceptions and the "consensus of informed observers" to arrive at a broad picture.

Fortunately, a consensus of informed observers does exist on a number of key facts. One is that substantial participation in key decision making is limited to a relatively small segment of the Jewish community (Medding 1981, 281). What is more, this leadership elite tends to be drawn from a relatively homogeneous population of the well-to-do and the well-connected (business people, professionals), with a sprinkling of academics and individuals with "Jewish credentials" (rabbis, Judaica scholars) thrown in.[2] Within the federation system, the members of the leadership group (which does, of course, vary in absolute size depending largely on the size of the Jewish community itself) tend to circulate among positions of influence, with many occupying several key positions (officer, committee chairperson, executive committee member) in the federation and its agencies simultaneously or successively. This, and the fact that leaders do tend to be drawn from the same strata often give the impression that the polity is governed by a kind of "interlocking directorate."

The existence of this governance elite—what Daniel Elazar, the American Jewish polity's most authoritative analyst, terms a "trusteeship of givers and doers" (1976, 336)—does not in itself, however, mean that the polity as a whole is either undemocratic or, as we shall see below, "un-Jewish." Several other factors must be considered. One is the question of how the elite achieves its position of power. Here, too, there is general agreement on the facts but less on their meaning. By and large, the members of the elite are coopted rather than selected by any grass-roots electoral process. Elections do take place, as we have noted. However, Elazar's assessment of their significance is amply supported: "Though not always formalities, [they] are usually simply means of formally ratifying the choices of nominating committees, and even when contested they are rarely contested by candidates representing seriously different characteristics or points of view" (Elazar 1976, 285).[3]

In this sense, it is fair to characterize the typical leadership pattern within the American Jewish polity as oligarchic. One must go further, however, and recognize that the leadership elite, although relatively small and not the product of democratic selection, is neither monolithic nor exclusive. The cosmopolitan volunteers who dominate federations and other Jewish communal organizations linked to the federation system do not constitute "an oligarchy that extends itself through all spheres of Jewish life" (Elazar 1976, 286). Synagogues, fraternal and membership organizations, and a host of other religious, educational, and special interest agencies within the Jewish community enjoy effective autonomy and are often led by rather different elements of the Jewish populace. With respect to the Jewish polity as a whole, leadership can be said to inhere in what Peter Medding calls a "multi-element oligarchy" in which elites "often coalesce rather than operate separately," at least within certain recognizable spheres of communal activity (1981, 283).

Even in regard to federations themselves, those who defend the current system against the charge of elite domination often point to the fact that far from seeking to exclude individuals from leadership opportunities, federations and their allied agencies are often engaged in a fruitless search for new volunteers willing and able to assume positions within the system. Sidney Vincent, one of the most thoughtful and influential leaders of the federation system in recent years, has written of this problem:

> All of us are committed to democracy by our entire training and our way of life. We mean it when we talk at our annual meetings about how eager we are for more participation by our citizenry, even in decision-making. But all democratic institutions struggle with the problem of how to involve their constituencies responsibly in decision-making. . . . In Jewish life, involvement is even harder to achieve. All our institutions are voluntary; very little is decided by general elections and no one needs to pay Jewish taxes. The great majority of our constituents know little or nothing about the great communal issues that absorb us. Indeed, the organized community is frequently perceived as a closed corporation, where the elite makes the decisions. Many of us vigorously refute that charge, claiming that the portals of entry into communal service and promotion are open to all those willing to devote themselves to communal service. To claim otherwise, we say, is a copout. . . [1982, 59].

Vincent's position is not without merit. Nearly every federation in the country maintains, as we shall discuss below, some form of leadership development program to recruit and train new candidates for leadership positions, and it is difficult to recount any instances where willing individuals have been turned away from entry-level responsibilities. As Elazar puts it, "The cosmopolitan voluntary leaders represent an oligarchy, but it is a voluntary one as much as or more than it is self-perpetuating" (1976, 286). Nevertheless, it is also important to note that the objective conditions required for entrance into the leadership elite—ability and willingness to expend sufficient time and energy on communal affairs, and a readiness to play by the "rules of the game," which emphasize avoidance of conflict— serve to eliminate or discourage many who might otherwise be both qualified and eager to have greater input into communal decision making. Wealth per se is not, as some critics have charged, either a requisite for or a guarantee of influence (in fact, top-level positions are only rarely filled by the wealthiest Jews in a community). But, given the importance of fund-raising for the federation system, it is not surprising that most leaders are drawn from the ranks of contributors whose gifts are substantial, if not necessarily enormous.[4]

Representativeness of Leaders

Critics and other observers of the communal system have often disputed the extent to which the leadership elite is representative of and fairly represents the Jewish community as a whole. For those like Shapiro, the answer is clear: "It is too obvious that the goals of the people and of Federation leadership are by now far apart" (Shapiro 1973, 204). Raphael, citing evidence from Columbus, Ohio, reaches a similar conclusion: contributor preferences are largely ignored when allocations committees do their work (1979, 155-63). Yet, there is substantial evidence, both impressionistic and empirical, to support an alternative perspective: Organizational leaders are by and large representative of their ostensible constituents; indeed, if they are unrepresentative, it is in maintaining higher levels of Jewish activism and concern. Based on data from the National Jewish Population Study conducted in 1970-71, Alan York concludes that a broad sample of Jewish leaders "participate more than non-leaders in Jewish organizations, they tend to give more to charity, to have higher occupational status, and to attend synagogue more frequently, but they are neither marginal in their Jewish practice and identification nor exceptional: they are as observant and identifying as the average American Jew" (1981, 25-36). Melvin Urofsky summarizes the results of his study as follows: "Today's leaders are not atypical of their followers, but archetypical" (1981, 406).

Even when one focuses specifically on the "cosmopolitan volunteers" who lead the federations and other major institutions of the Jewish polity, the situation seems much the same. Elazar writes that "the trusteeship is representative of American Jewry in that it reflects the attitudes, values, and interests of the community—except perhaps in one respect: the leaders are probably more positively Jewish than the community's rank and file" (1974, 109). Charles Liebman, indeed, describes the leaders of New York's Federation of Jewish Philanthropies, the largest federation in the United States, as "not representative of New York's Jews, or of Federation's own

contributors" precisely because "by and large, they are more Jewishly concerned and committed" (1979, 65). Several surveys of leaders of national
Jewish organizations and of federation activists conducted in recent years
have confirmed this finding: leaders have on average higher levels of Jewish
identification (ritual observance included) than do Jews as a whole
(Woocher 1981a, 1981b; Cohen 1983; Cohen and Woocher 1982).

Part of the debate over leadership representativeness is rooted in the
ambiguity of the concept itself. At least three models of political representation can be identified: (1) the representative as "mirror image" of his/her
constituency; (2) the representative as "trustee" (exercising his/her own
best judgment on behalf of the constituency); and (3) the representative as
"surrogate" (acting as the constituents presumably would, had they the
same knowledge as the representative does) (Jones 1970, 38-42). Polity
leaders act primarily as representatives in the second sense, i.e. as trustees.
Whether that is the appropriate model for the Jewish community can
surely be debated. It is not clear, however, whether the expectations of
critics that a shift to an alternative model would produce substantially
different—or from their point of view preferable—outcomes would be confirmed.[5] The few studies that have been done, e.g. of contributor preferences for the expenditure of federation funds, have produced ambiguous
results.[6] Because the leadership elite is itself not monolithic in its attitudes,
it is likely that most significant points of view are represented, though
perhaps not in proportion to their weight within the Jewish populace as a
whole.

Communication and Accountability: The Critical Issues

One might justifiably conclude that the narrow base of participation in
decision making and the lack of meaningful input by the larger community
in the selection of leaders are not in and of themselves fatal barriers to the
leadership's capacity to fulfill the representative function that democratic
theory demands. In other respects, however, the system that the critics of
the past two decades have described does fall well short of a democratic
ideal. The most serious liability, many would agree, is the lack of mechanisms for providing regular communication between the leadership elite
and the community rank and file. Accurate representation of constituency
preferences, when it occurs, is more the result of the lack of serious ideological diversity within the American Jewish community than of deliberate efforts to channel constituent concerns to leadership cadres.

Again, this is not, by and large, due to a desire to ignore such expres-
sions. Rather, it is the lack of initiatives by either the leaders or the average
members of the community that is so debilitating. The problem is in part

structural—formal channels of access are either nonexistent or ineffi-
cient—but it is also more broadly systemic. Medding notes that, especially
at national levels of policy-making.

> there exist no democratic or representative integrative mechanisms for join-
> ing rank and file members to their leaders. . . . The views, ideas, goals and
> aspirations of the Jewish grass roots and rank and file reach the top, if at all,
> only as interpreted and presented by various sub-leaders who, presumably,
> have their own personal and institutional interests to promote, which must
> clearly influence their transmission of the views of their constituents [1981,
> 277-79].

The major problem, however, goes beyond these structural limitations.
The American Jewish polity suffers from a paucity of what Elazar calls
"publics," groups of Jews actively committed to participation in communal affairs on an ongoing basis. It is this lack that men like Sidney Vincent
point to when they cite open doors through which no one is walking. It is
not a question here of a total absence of inputs to and demands on the
political system. Individuals and institutions do come with their positions
and concerns. But they do so often as pressure groups and self-proclaimed
populists, almost in a posture of antagonism, rather than as elements in a
set of publics prepared to engage in an orderly process of interest aggrega-
tion and representation (Elazar 1982, 10-11; Stern 1982, 111-15).

The problem is both one of the quantity of participation and of its
quality. With neither a tradition of nor mechanisms for regular debate on
matters of policy and program, leaders tend to hear either opinions that
only confirm the established consensus or opposing views that represent a
disturbance of that consensus and hence may be both offered and received
in a quasi-confrontational atmosphere. Where to place blame for this state
of affairs is largely a moot point; clearly, a vicious cycle can take, and
probably has taken, hold. What is evident is, that as Elazar warns, a "re-
publican" system of communal governance cannot long endure without
"publics" prepared and permitted to take part in its affairs as a matter of
course (1982, 4).

The depressed level of public participation and access also undercuts the
possibility of establishing genuine accountability among the leadership for
its decisions. Once more, it is not that leaders wish to arrogate all power to
their own hands and to ignore the community's interests. However, even
sincere trustees require some mechanisms for determining when policies
are in fact meeting with the approval of and meeting the needs of the
community whom they seek to serve. Without contested elections or broad
public participation in decision making, such mechanisms are lacking and
accountability is theoretical rather than operational.

Leadership elites believe that they are acting responsively and responsibly, but the only way of judging whether this is so is the rather crude measure provided by annual fund-raising campaigns. Even by this criterion, it is not clear that the Jewish populace at large is satisfied with either the substance or process of communal decision making, but efforts to increase direct accountability for specific policy choices are almost nonexistent. The ultimate danger for the community in the distance that exists between leadership and constituency is that the community at some point simply will be unable to mobilize the relatively apathetic masses for even the minimal levels of support that are necessary for the communal enterprise itself to endure. In this sense, greater democracy (as we have defined it) is not merely a normative ideal but a requisite for the polity's survival. As Medding puts it: "Whether Jewish communities, organized as they currently are, and without more responsive and representative leadership and executive bodies, will continue to be able to mobilize the vast majority of members of Jewish communities and command their loyalty is an open question" (1981, 285).

Steps toward Democratization

The concern Medding noted finds echoes even within the leadership establishment itself. In the decade and a half since the last wave of critics began their assault on the communal system, the situation decried then has not remained static. Transformations in both the composition of the leadership cadres and, to a more limited extent, in the processes of communal governance have taken place that have affected the state of democracy within the polity. These changes have not all been deliberate, nor have they necessarily taken place with democratization as their goal. In fact, as we shall see, their impact in this respect has been somewhat ambiguous. But they do constitute the polity's best efforts thus far to respond to the implicit warning in assessments like that of Medding, and they do establish the direction along which future changes are likely to take place.

We should initially note three areas of change in the recruitment, composition, and characteristics of the leadership elite in recent years. The first are efforts to recruit and advance leaders from previously underrepresented segments of the community. Three groups in particular have been targeted (in some instances following or concurrent with their own demands for greater representation): youth, women, and the Orthodox. The success of these efforts has been mixed. A number of women have broken out of their segregation in "women's divisions" to become presidents of federations (in such major communities as New York, Boston, and Baltimore), campaign chairpersons, and, most recently, heads of major national agencies (the Jewish Welfare Board and the National Jewish

Community Relations Advisory Council). Representation of women on major committees and in other positions of responsibility does appear to have increased. Further, new provisions are being made to recruit and involve professional and business women (alongside women who are now often called "professional volunteers") in ways roughly equivalent to those targeted at their male counterparts. Whether these changes have brought new viewpoints into leadership circles is less certain, but they have symbolized an opening of the elite across what has heretofore been one of its major boundaries (Lipstadt 1980).

Efforts to involve larger numbers of young people, from whose ranks many of the establishment's most vocal critics were drawn, have been, on the whole, less successful. A number of federations and other organizations have made places on their boards and committees for youth and student representation. Many have increased their allocations or programming for what are defined as student- or youth-oriented concerns.[7] These steps have not, however, brought more than a handful of those under the age of twenty-five into active participation. The focus of polity outreach has been on a somewhat older and, realistically, more potentially productive group—those referred to as "young leadership," between the ages of twenty-five and forty (see the discussion below).

The third group that has been both a critic and more recently a recruitment target of the polity establishment is the Orthodox community. For many years the federation was regarded as a "secular" institution led largely by assimilated Reform Jews. In more recent decades the latter proposition has lost its validity as Conservative Jews have come to share leadership positions alongside those who identify with the Reform movement.[8] The former characterization as well, as we shall note below, is increasingly inappropriate, but what has remained true until quite recently is that few Jews who identified themselves as Orthodox were in positions of lay or professional leadership in the federation system. It is difficult to know to what extent this situation has changed. It is clear that many federations have become more responsive to concerns traditionally identified with the Orthodox community, e.g., support for Jewish day schools (although this also reflects the overall Judaization of the polity discussed below). Very recently some signs of a countermovement have developed, with increasing complaints being heard that "concessions" to the Orthodox have not produced a concomitant increase in their commitment and contributions to federation. At the same time, some Orthodox and other denominational leaders continue to decry what they perceive as tokenism in both the involvement of and responsiveness to the religious community.

There has, then, been a gradual broadening of the leadership elite of the polity in recent years, with greater opportunities for participation by mem-

bers of underrepresented segments of the community. Even where decision-making power is still largely in the hands of more traditional
leadership types, the meeting of demand and outreach has produced some
corollary advances in the democratization process. Better communication
has been established with these constituencies (youth and the Orthodox
tend to be better organized as such than are women). In addition, polity
agencies do feel a stronger sense of accountability to these groups, even
where mechanisms for ensuring that they are actually held accountable are
missing.

Judaization of the Polity and Socialization of the Leadership

In assessing the impact of the changes discussed above, one must take
account of two other processes that have been occurring simultaneously.
The first of these, alluded to previously, is a general Judaization of the
polity. This constitutes the latest phase in the longer-term consolidation of
the polity's "civil religion" of "Jewish survivalism" (Woocher 1979, 1981a,
1981c). As a worldview and ethos, this civil religion focuses on countering
threats to Jewish continuity, security, and well-being while promoting an
ethic of exemplary Jewish moral responsibility. Whereas it was once possible to find Jewish communal leaders whose basic ideological commitment
was to "the melting pot," to "charitable work," or to an ideal of "universal
social justice," these values have now been subordinated (where they remain present at all) to the overriding values of Jewish survival and mutual
responsibility. As the comments above concerning the levels of Jewish
commitment found among leadership cadres indicate, recent years have
seen a movement toward greater congruence between public ideology and
personal behavior as the civil religion, with its utilization and positive
valuation of Jewish myth, symbol, and ritual forms, has taken hold. What
has emerged is a new model for the Jewish polity leader: one who works for
the continuity of the Jewish people and its tradition in every arena—the
personal-familial, the communal-institutional, and the public-political.

Helping to propel the spread of this new model, and thereby of the
polity's Judaization, is the third major area of recent change in the realm of
leadership: the dramatic spread of institutionalized programs for the recruitment and socialization of new leaders. Leadership-development programs are now a staple not only of federations but of nearly every major
national Jewish organization. Often these programs serve as one means of
bringing women, Orthodox, and other "atypical" Jews into the leadership
pipeline. They are also the prime means of trying to induce younger business and professional leaders to follow in the footsteps of their active elders.
But even more, and in some respects countering the democratizing influ-

ence of such programs, they socialize these young leaders into the regnant Jewish-survivalist ideology. Participants in the programs are sensitized to critical Jewish issues, oriented to the agencies and the way they operate, and given increasingly important roles in carrying on the work of the polity. Young-leadership cadres have had an impact on the federation world in spearheading the movement toward greater Judaization and a broader definition of leadership responsibilities. In so doing, they have become an elite within the elite, in many ways even less representative of the community at large than their elders.

Dilemmas of Democratization

Here we confront again one of the major dilemmas in any discussion of democratization of the American Jewish community. Taken literally, such a program might well involve a slowing or even a reversal of the trends toward heightened Jewishness among polity leaders. Yet somewhere between a project of this type, which even most critics would view with great skepticism, and the current trend toward the promotion of a more Jewishly concerned, but ideologically homogeneous, leadership, there may well be a system for recruiting and training leadership that would bring positive, but diverse, Jewish commitments into the polity and would allow this wider range of commitments to inform the polity's self-definition and policy deliberations. For all of its merits, the Jewish survivalism that dominates the attitudes of current and emerging leaders alike is an ideology that supports rather than challenges the already powerful consensual biases of the communal governance system.

In fact, the powerful emphasis within communal rhetoric on unity and on adopting a communitywide perspective on problems has probably resulted in some dilution of the representational aspects of the system. Whereas it was once not uncommon for individuals to speak on behalf of particular agencies, interests, or ideologies within decision-making councils, this type of representation appears to be diminishing. Instead, leaders seek to anticipate the "community consensus" that presumably represents a synthesis of all interests and viewpoints. This high-mindedness reflects the fact that there is, as we have seen, a broad consensus on many issues, certainly among the leadership cadres, but it also tends to foreclose vigorous debate and makes aggressive representation and subcommunal interests appear somewhat suspect. Many instances have been recounted of occasions when issues have seemingly been decided by majority votes, only to have the winners draw back because the decision did not command a full consensus. The quest for consensus is, on the one hand, a sound and democratic means of insuring that minority viewpoints are protected. It can, however, also be debilitating for the democratic process, forcing premature compromise and pushing truly dissenting viewpoints outside the process altogether.

The Expanding Polity Agenda and a Maturing Self-Awareness

In raising this issue of how increasing ideological homogeneity can work subtly to weaken some of the representational elements built into the polity's governance process, we should not overlook other changes that may be counterbalancing this effect. One of these is the expansion of the public agenda of Jewish communal life itself. In recent years more and more areas of Jewish activity have come to be seen as requiring public attention, as opposed to being left for individual or private institutional action alone. The polity is now called upon to be increasingly involved in Jewish education, in the quality of Jewish family life, in the support of religious activities, and in public affairs. These new responsibilities are in many ways an outgrowth of the survivalist ideology we have discussed above. Their pursuit has required that the polity interact with a wider range of Jews than in the days when it was primarily devoted to providing health, welfare, and recreational services. Synagogue leaders, day school supporters, children of young parents, Jewish political activists, and others who previously were not foci of attention and concern are now perceived as constituencies that must be incorporated in some fashion within the polity.

The desire to involve new segments of the community in the overall communal system is most apparent in the frequent discussions among leaders of the need to "reach out to the unaffiliated." Most polity leaders are well aware of the fact that a substantial majority of Jews are only tenuously (if at all) involved in the Jewish communal network. The desire to bring these marginal Jews into the system is in many respects a survival requisite for the system, as implied by Medding above. But the motivation for outreach efforts is idealistic as well. Polity leaders believe in the concept of community, and their concern for the future of Jewish life is both genuine and personal. What have not yet been developed are strategies and techniques of outreach that are effective in bringing in the unaffiliated. Most continue to seek to develop better understanding of the system and its goals, which will presumably lead to commitment, and eventually to participation. Only quite recently have new approaches begun to be attempted that seek to appeal to the unaffiliated in terms of their specific concerns and patterns of involvement, which may or may not be similar to those already active within the Jewish polity. Finding different points of access and new types of participation for the currently unaffiliated, perhaps even the development of new structures—with the assumption that commitment may follow upon rather than precede such involvement—is a major challenge to the polity just beginning to be addressed.[9]

The final, and perhaps ultimately the most important, factor in propelling the American Jewish community toward greater democratization today is the growing awareness of its own political character. The idea that the Jewish organizational matrix constitutes a polity has never been entirely absent from its self-consciousness. Nor did concern for its democratic character await this awareness. But the greater sensitivity of leaders to the fact that they are engaged in a political process, and a growing sophistication in their understanding of how the nature of this process relates to the success of their endeavors focus attention on the issues of access, participation, representation, decision making, and accountability that we have emphasized above. The gradual redefinition of the polity mission from service provision alone to community development helps to engender this heightened political consciousness.

Assessing the State of Polity Democracy

It may now be possible to venture some answers to the questions posed earlier: Are federations—and the Jewish polity in general—democratic? More so than they have been in the past, we would suggest, and less so than they could be. To what extent is democracy an appropriate form of Jewish communal governance today? If by *democracy* we mean a system that provides substantial opportunities for access and participation by all those who seek involvement, in which there are some mechanisms for representing diverse interests and viewpoints, in which policy alternatives are openly debated, in which leaders are accountable for their actions, and in which efforts are made to develop publics and enhance the quality of citizen participation in political processes, then we would answer that communal democracy is a valid goal.

In offering these judgments we must, at the same time, offer several qualifications. What seems neither feasible nor desirable in American Jewish life are some of the more radical schemes for democratization that have been suggested. National representative bodies, or even communal elections on a local scale, seem unlikely to prove workable in the foreseeable future. As Elazar notes, and Medding's researches confirm (1981, 279-80),

> Those modern Jewish communities which have experimented with communal elections have not found them any better a solution to the problem of representation, because the turnout in these elections tends to be extremely low. Moreover, a voting procedure does not guarantee the election of statesmen to communal leadership either [Elazar 1974, 109].

As long as the American Jewish polity is a voluntary one, with a multiplicity of organizations, there will probably always be a tendency for central or framing institutions like the federations to place a high premium on the maintenance of consensus and the avoidance of conflict. Other arenas exist for those who wish to pursue particular interests and concerns in the many subcommunal organizations. Thus, vigorous contest over policy or office at the core of the polity is unlikely to become the norm, and the U.S. model of representative democracy is likely to remain an inapt one for the Jewish community.

Even more important, perhaps, the political tradition of the Jewish people, one that has served it well across a broad expanse of time and space, is not itself a radical democratic one. Rather, it rests on a philosophy that Elazar has labeled "aristocratic republicanism" and that Mordecai Roshwald has called "democratic elitism" (Elazar 1982; Roshwald 1978). The polity belongs to the people, not to its rulers, but actual leadership is vested in a group of trustees—responsible both to the people and Jewish law—who are selected on the basis of their qualification to serve. As Elazar describes it,

> Political life in Jewish communities and polities has usually involved the following factors: (1) the initial consent of the members to the community's authority and to the authoritative structures and processes of governance within it; (2) a commitment toward participation in communal affairs on the part of a relatively substantial percentage of the citizenry; (3) the utilization of various forms of representation . . . where direct participation was not feasible; and (4) a system of dispersed decision-making with different tasks assigned to different bodies often involving the same individuals wearing many different hats, moving from body to body in their leadership capacities [1981, 49-50].

In broad terms, the American Jewish polity today works within this framework, and the criteria it suggests seem appropriate ones for evaluating the polity's continued progress toward the proper blend of democratic and aristocratic principles.

Avenues for Democratization

There are avenues along which democratization can and should proceed that would conform with both the limits imposed by the environment within which American Jewish organizations must operate and the norms of the Jewish political tradition. Many are relatively simple to conceive, though perhaps more difficult to execute: rotation of officeholders, creation of formal channels for receiving "citizen" input, more vigorous efforts to educate and inform the Jewish community about issues and the political process, insurance that no single criterion—such as wealth—becomes the sole qualifying factor for recruitment into the leadership elite.

More far-reaching measures can also be envisioned. Elazar, for example, has suggested that drawing the synagogues more directly into the public domain might provide a basis for an electoral process through congregations that would enhance the representative character of federation leadership and provide new sources for recruitment (1976, 337-38). Nearly all critics, observers, and defenders of the current system alike agree that the prime requisite today is to increase participation in communal affairs by the Jewish rank and file. This means not only proclaiming the system's openness but providing incentives and new structural designs for such involvement. Here, current experiments with such "constitutional" changes as regionalization, mail ballots to elect a portion of governing boards, and various proportional representation schemes, may be pointing the way forward.[10]

In the final analysis, the transformations that have taken place in American Jewish communal governance over the past several decades may not appear dramatic, but they are nonetheless real and potentially significant. American Jews are engaged in a historic venture: trying to maintain a voluntary political system that responds to the traditional demand for Jewish survival and the modern demand for democratic governance. Whether and how they succeed in that endeavor will provide lessons not only for other Jews but for all those interested in the dynamics of political organization in modern societies.

Notes

1. In adopting the federation system as the focal point of our examination, we must offer an important caveat. The governance system of the American Jewish polity is extraordinarily complex and variegated. The polity itself is in many ways more an intellectual construct than a functioning reality; this is certainly so for many of its "citizens." It is a matrix of diverse institutions and organizations, all voluntary, most operating independently of one another in a variety of arenas ranging from the neighborhood to the world. The polity has no formal center, no overall leadership, no overarching structure. If we choose to concentrate in the discussion below on Jewish federations, it is because by common consent they are the most—but certainly not the only—important elements in the organizational matrix. To a large extent, because the American Jewish community generally shares a single political culture, the comments and observations made below will be applicable to more than just the federation sphere. That domain will, however, be the focal point of concern here, and because generalization even within that sphere is risky, it is all the more so beyond its boundaries.

2. Two major studies of federation leadership in specific communities were conducted in the 1960s by Arnold Gurin (Detroit) and Kenneth Roseman (Cincinnati). Neither has been published in full, but excerpts have appeared in Raphael (1979). The most recent large-scale study of community leadership was conducted by Charles Liebman (1979), and focused on the leadership of the New York Federation of Jewish Philanthropies.

    One should, perhaps, also include the cadre of professional Jewish communal workers, especially agency executives, within the leadership elite. A number of observers regard these professionals as the single most influential force in communal governance. (See, e.g., Shapiro [1973] and a number of articles in Raphael [1979].) The question is whether these professionals constitute a democratizing force within the polity. Some do indeed come from social strata and religious backgrounds not well represented among the volunteer leadership, but it is unclear whether this has any substantive impact on their policy preferences or attitudes on communal process. More relevant, in all likelihood, is their professional training and identification, which may make them somewhat more sensitive than lay leaders to varying viewpoints but emphasizes a facilitative rather than advocacy role within the system.

3. The one major organization in the American Jewish community that prides itself on holding contested elections for the office of international president—B'nai B'rith—illustrates this point. It is unusually difficult, if not impossible, to find any significant differences, either in background or general policy orientation, among the several candidates.

4. Today's rhetoric emphasizes the need to make a "quality" gift in proportion to one's means. Nevertheless, a measure of affluence remains an almost necessary if insufficient condition for leadership advancement, both because it helps to insure that the "quality" of one's gift is noted and because fulfilling communal responsibilities often involves travel, time taken from work, and other ancillary expenses that require disposable income.

5. This should not be taken as implying that contributor and constituent preferences ought to play no role in determining policies and priorities. One of the difficulties in this regard is developing appropriate ways of presenting policy options or priorities (e.g. in federation allocations) to the Jewish public. Allocations are made to agencies and programs, not to goals and priorities, and determining how the two are related in specific terms is often a difficult matter of analysis and judgment. The application of public opinion polling and market-research techniques to Jewish communal affairs is only in its nascent stages in the United States, and its potential impact on decision making and communal democracy is unknown.

6. Cf. Raphael (1979), who reports a significant difference between rank-and-file donor preferences and the actual allocation of federation funds in Columbus, Ohio, with Weinberger (1971), who found substantial consensus on priorities among donors and allocators in San Diego, California.

7. The North American Jewish Students Appeal, which receives allocations from many federations and supports a number of student-oriented projects, is one example of this. The increasing role of federations in funding Hillel Foundations and other student activities has naturally raised questions of cooptation and tokenism. Some student groups prefer to remain outside the "system" in order to maintain their autonomy.

8. The author's research on young leadership groups indicates that Jews who call themselves "Conservative" may be on the way to assuming a preponderant role in federation leadership circles.
9. One recent effort in this direction is the New Gifts Program of the United Jewish Appeal, which is attempting to supplement traditional approaches to fund-raising by utilizing state-of-the-art attitudinal research and marketing methods.
10. The process of democratization would benefit from a coordinated effort to collate and evaluate the initiatives developed by the various local communities in this direction. Of local efforts thus far initiated, those in Los Angeles, which has developed a major regionalization program, appear to be both the most sophisticated and carefully evaluated. The highly decentralized structure of the American Jewish polity serves both as a boon by permitting experimentation on a modest scale and as a barrier by making communication of the results of such experiments more difficult.

References

Cohen, Steven M. 1983. "Attitudes of American Jews Toward Israel and Israelis." New York: Institute on American Jewish-Israeli Relations, American Jewish Committee.
_____, and Jonathan Woocher. 1982. "American Jewish Leadership Survey." Unpublished.
Dahl, Robert. 1956. *A Preface to Democratic Theory.* Chicago: University of Chicago Press.
Elazar, Daniel J. 1970. *Cities of the Prairie.* New York: Basic Books.
_____. 1974. "Decision-making in the American Jewish Community." In *The Jewish Community in America,* ed. Marshall Sklare, pp. 72-110. New York: Behrman House.
_____. 1976. *Community and Polity: The Organizational Dynamics of American Jewry.* Philadelphia: Jewish Publication Society.
_____. 1981. "Covenant as the basis of the Jewish Political Tradition." In *Kinship and Consent: The Jewish Political Tradition and Its Contemporary Uses,* ed. Daniel J. Elazar, pp. 21-56. Ramat-Gan and Philadelphia: Turtledove.
_____. 1982. *Participation and Accountability in the Jewish Community.* New York: Council of Jewish Federations and Association of Jewish Community Organization Personnel.
Jones, Charles O. 1970. *An Introduction to the Study of Public Policy.* Belmont, Calif.: Duxbury Press.
Levine, Hillel. 1973. "To Share a Vision." In *Jewish Radicalism,* ed. Jack Nusan Porter and Peter Dreier, pp. 183-94. New York: Grove Press.
Liebman, Charles S. 1979. "Leadership and Decision-making in a Jewish Federation: The New York Federation of Jewish Philanthropies." In *American Jewish Year Book* 79: 3-76.
Lipstadt, Deborah. 1980. "The Changing Nature of Power and Policy Making in the American Jewish Community: The Case of Women." Unpublished.
Medding, Peter. 1981. "Patterns of Political Organization and Leadership in Contemporary Jewish Communities." In *Kinship and Consent: The Jewish Politi-*

cal Tradition and Its Contemporary Uses, ed. Daniel J. Elazar, 259-88. Ramat-Gan and Philadelphia: Turtledove.

Raphael, Marc Lee. 1979. "Federated Jewish Philanthropy and Communal Democracy: In Pursuit of a Phantom." In *Understanding American Jewish Philanthropy,* ed. Marc Lee Raphael, 153-63. New York: Ktav.

Roshwald, Mordecai. 1978. "Democratic Elitism: The Ideological Framework of Jewish Community." *Judaism* 27 (Winter): 47-62.

Shapiro, Judah J. 1973. "The Philistine Philanthropists: The Power and Shame of Jewish Federations." In *Jewish Radicalism,* ed. Jack Nusan Porter and Peter Dreier, pp. 201-8. New York: Grove Press.

Stern, Jay. 1982. "Some Thoughts on the Polity of Jewish Organizational Life." *Journal of Jewish Communal Service* 59 (Winter): 111-15.

Urofsky, Melvin I. 1981. "American Jewish Leadership." *American Jewish History* 70 (June): 406.

Vincent, Sidney. 1982. *Personal and Professional: Memoirs of a Life in Community Service.* Cleveland: Jewish Community Federation of Cleveland.

Weinberger, Paul. 1971. "An Empirical Assessment of Priorities in Jewish Community Services." *Journal of Jewish Communal Service* 48 (Winter): 159-66.

Woocher, Jonathan S. 1979. "Civil Judaism in the United States." Philadelphia: Center for Jewish Community Studies.

_____. 1981a. "The 'Civil Judaism' of Communal Leaders." In *American Jewish Year Book* 81: 149-69.

_____. 1981b. "The 1980 UJA Young Leadership Cabinet: A Profile." *Forum* 42/43 (Winter): 57-68.

_____. 1981c. "'Jewish Survivalism' as Communal Ideology: An Empirical Assessment." *Journal of Jewish Communal Service* 57 (Summer): 291-303.

York, Alan S. 1981. "American Jewish Leaders from the Periphery." *Jewish Journal of Sociology* 23 (June): 25-36.

RESEARCH NOTES

4

Sex Differences in Attitudes of American Jews toward Israel

Jay Y. Brodbar-Nemzer

Sex differences in the attitudes of American Jews are explored in an attempt to increase our understanding of American Jewish identity and the political attitudes of American Jewish women. Using the 1981-1982 National Survey of American Jews, we find comparable levels of positive attitudes toward Israel between men and women. Women, however, were more likely to support Israeli policy. They were less likely to view the Israeli government as too hawkish, less willing to engage in public criticism, and less likely to favor the return of territory for peace. These differences are surprising in light of the general trend among American women to hold more dovish attitudes. The differences remain after controlling for a host of background and theoretically related variables. The results are discussed in light of recent discussions of doves and hawks and Israeli policy.

Introduction

The study of sex differences in the political attitudes of American Jews toward Israel is important because it addresses one of the primary loci of American Jewish identity and helps to fill a major gap in the literature. The relative neglect of the political attitudes and behavior of women generally has been a focus of a fair amount of treatment (Frankovic 1982), but political attitudes of American Jewish women have received little attention. Recently Welch and Ullrich (1984) made an initial attempt at rectifying this situation. In this analysis we will augment our understanding of the political attitudes of American Jewish women by exploring an arena that Welch and Ullrich (1984;54) themselves recognize as a lacuna in their own analysis—the attitudes of American Jewish women toward Israel.

There are several reasons that attitudes toward Israel, especially sex differences in such attitudes, are of interest. First, sex differences among

American Jews in their attitudes toward Israel would inform the general concern with sex differences in political behavior. Those studies reviewing sex differences in Americans' political behavior since World War II do find one consistent sex difference: women are more likely than men to be doves (Mueller 1973; *Public Opinion* 1982a; Frankovic 1982).[1]

Second, comparable to the long-term neglect of sex differences in political attitudes in general, and of Jews specifically, there has been an interest in redressing the neglect of sex differences in the study of religiosity and religious identity (Vernon and Cardwell 1980). The general trend has been that women report consistently higher levels of religiosity than men (Argyle and Beit-Hallahmi 1975; Batson and Ventis 1982; Vernon and Cardwell 1980). Recently Israel has become increasingly important as a component of American Jewish identity (Hertzberg 1979). Although modern Zionist ideology has been perceived to be a largely secular phenomenon, stressing the national basis of Jewish identity, the link to the State of Israel has come to represent an important aspect of "the content or the expression of Jewish religious identity" (Liebman 1973; 88). The spring of 1967 has been seen as a period of transformation, when Israel became an important basis of American Jewish solidarity and Jewish identity (Hertzberg 1979). Indeed, Liebman (1973; 90-91) has argued that support of Israel has become the normative "boundary defining position in the communal consensus of American Jews." Empirically, Sklare and Greenblum (1979) and Cohen (1982) have demonstrated the widespread concern for Israel among American Jewry. Thus, explorations into sex differences in attitudes toward Israel can be seen as an inquiry into sex differences in Jewish identity itself.

When we try to predict sex differences in the political attitudes of American Jews with respect to Israel in light of the above, we see that the picture is not completely clear. On the one hand, we could expect that in concert with overall societal trends, Jewish women would be inclined to espouse dovish sentiments with respect to Israel. On the other hand, if Jewish women were to be seen as more closely identified and committed to Judaism and Jewish peoplehood, their attitudes might be more hawkish than the attitudes of Jewish men. Thus, American Jewish women could be seen as being pulled in two contradictory directions: a dovishness in keeping with general societal sex differences or a relative hawkishness that underscores a commitment to and an insecurity about the survival of the State of Israel. In this analysis we shall investigate empirically sex differences in the attitudes of American Jews toward Israel in an attempt to understand these cross pressures and to add to our rather scanty knowledge of the political attitudes of American Jewish women.

Data Source and Findings

I will explore the role of gender using the 1981-1982 National Survey of American Jews (Cohen 1982). The sample was selected using the Distinctive Jewish Names technique[2] and was constructed so as to approximate the geographic distribution of American Jews as reported in the 1980 *American Jewish Year Book*. Based on telephone directory listings from over forty communities, 1,700 questionnaires were initially mailed during the fall of 1981.[3] An estimated 300 were ineligible (non-Jewish) or returned as undeliverable; and slightly less than half ($N = 673$) of the pool of 1,400 potential eligible respondents completed the questionnaire by February 1982. Based on his comparison of demographic and other variables with the results of other studies of American Jewry, Cohen (1982) concludes that these data are likely to be fairly accurate representations of the American Jewish community at large. My analysis of sex differences will be based on the responses of the 358 males and 305 females who participated in the study.[4]

In his analyses of these data, Cohen (1982) introduced a crucial distinction with respect to supportive attitudes toward Israel. He argued that one must distinguish between broad support and concern for Israel versus support for Israeli government policy. Thus, he found in this same sample, high levels of support for Israel. For example, 83 percent agreed that "if Israel were destroyed, I would feel as if I had suffered one of the greatest personal tragedies in my life," and 94 percent viewed themselves as "pro" or "very-pro" Israel (Cohen 1982; 95). On the other hand, when one looks at attitudes toward Israeli government policy there is much less consensus. For example, the sample splits evenly, 41 percent agreeing and 41 percent disagreeing with the statement "If Israel could be assured of peace and secure borders, she should be willing to return to Arab control most of the territories she has occupied since 1967." Additionally, nearly a quarter of the respondents may be classified as doves on the Middle East, characterizing "Israel's policies in its disputes with Arabs" as "too hawkish" (Cohen 1982; 97). Thus, it seems that wide support for Israel (what Cohen termed "concern") is not necessarily indicative of endorsement of Israeli government policy.

Table 4.1 presents the responses to various attitudinal items by sex. The first group of items taps what Cohen (1982) called a "concern" for Israel. In general, these nine items reveal similar high levels of concern for Israel among both American Jewish males and females. For example, on the general item that assesses one's attitude toward Israel, fully 92 percent of the males and 96 percent of the females classify themselves as "pro-" or "very pro-Israel." The other items reflect a similar general pattern for men and women of comparable levels of concern. The only substantial difference concerns voting for candidates unfriendly to Israel. Women are more likely than men to endorse the concept of not voting for candidates unfriendly to Israel, by a margin of 82 percent to 70 percent. I shall return to this item shortly.

The next group of items measures attitudes toward Israeli policy. As reported above, Cohen found the distinction between broad concern and support for the state versus support for specific policies and a particular government's actions as an important one. The first three items in this group follow the trend noted above: comparable levels of support on the part of both women and men. However, a significant difference emerges in the last three items in table 4.1. Women are less willing to return territories after an assurance of peace (49 percent versus 34 percent).[5] They are also more likely than men to endorse the concept of not criticizing Israel publicly (44 percent versus 32 percent). Finally, when we turn to the question of the respondent's general assessment of Israeli policy toward the Arabs, we find that men are more likely than women to view that policy critically, terming it too "hawkish" (28 percent versus 17 percent).

Thus, although a comparably high level of concern toward Israel exists among American Jewish women and men, it seems that women are more likely to support Israeli government policy: they are less likely to view it as too hawkish, less willing to engage in public criticism, and less likely to endorse the return of territory for peace. Although it is difficult to separate an endorsement of the policies of a particular government from an endorsement of the actions of the Israeli government in general, it would be accurate to place women, based on this pattern of results, closer to the Israeli government position of that time.

It is also interesting to note that the earlier difference on the voting item is consistent with this pattern. What is emerging is a picture of American Jewish women as being as highly concerned as men about Israel, but slightly more likely to endorse Israeli policy on a general level, and more likely to translate that concern and endorsement into the type of action that includes not voting for candidates perceived as unfriendly to Israel and not criticizing Israeli policy publicly.

Thus, it appears that with respect to Israel, American Jewish women's attitudes run counter to women's general inclination toward relative dovishness. How do we explain this sex difference on the policy dimension? Let us examine it while holding constant other relevant variables. First, it is interesting that this sex difference also runs counter to the fact that liberals are less supportive of Israeli policy (Cohen 1982) and that in these data

TABLE 4.1
Attitudes of American Jews toward Israel, by Sex

Attitudes	Male	Female
Of general concern and support		
In general, how would you characterize your feelings about Israel . . .		
% Very pro-Israel	43	44
% Pro-Israel	49	52
% Neutral	7	4
% Anti-Israel	2	1
Importance of security of Israel as an issue confronting American Jews (% "very important")	65	72
Israel's future is secure (% disagree)	68	74
Each American Jew should give serious thought to settling in Israel (% agree)	14	9
I often talk about Israel with friends and relatives (% agree)	66	68
There are times when my devotion to Israel comes into conflict with my devotion to America (% disagree)	72	72
If Israel were destroyed, I would feel as if I had suffered one of the greatest personal tragedies in my life (% agree)	81	84
Jews should not vote for candidates who are unfriendly to Israel (% agree)	70	82
U.S. support for Israel is in America's interest (% agree)	95	92
Attitudes toward Israeli policy		
Israel is right not to agree to sit down with the Palestine Liberation Organization (PLO), because the PLO is a terrorist organization that wants to destroy Israel (% agree)	74	73
If the alternatives are permanent Israeli annexation of the West Bank or an independent Palestinian state, then an independent Palestinian state is preferable (% disagree)	41	42
If the West Bank became an independent Palestinian state, it would probably be used as a launching pad to endanger Israel (% agree)	63	65
If Israel could be assured of peace and secure borders, she should be willing to return to Arab control most of the territories she had occupied since 1967 (% disagree)	34	49
American Jews should not criticize Israel's policies publicly (% agree)	32	44
In general . . . Israel's policies in its dispute with the Arabs have been		
% Too "hawkish"	28	17
% About right: not too "hawkish" or too "dovish"	69	79
% Too "dovish"	4	4
Median N^a	(348)	(293)

Note: Response categories reflect a disposition to support Israel and current Israeli government policies.

[a]Range: males, 343-355; females, 277-303.

women are more liberal, both in terms of self-identification and of attitudes on domestic issues and presidential voting.

Table 4.2 considers this pattern of sex differences while controlling for levels of liberalism. Inspection of this table reveals that the sex difference still remains. Thus, even among those scoring high in liberalism—those who are least hawkish—women are still more likely than men to hold pro-Israeli policy views.

Perhaps women's higher level of support might be explained by their greater Jewish involvement. Thus, as indicated earlier, if we would expect women to be more Jewishly active and identified, and if Israel plays a part in American Jewish identity, we would expect higher levels of endorsement of these items by women. It is puzzling that women did not score substantially higher on the concern items. It is possible that given the strong consensus on general concern for Israel, sex does not emerge as a differentiating factor. It is only on the level of policy that such differences emerge. Inspection of table 4.2, however, reveals that sex differences in ritual observance do not account for the sex differences on policy issues. We see, once more, that the relationship between sex and these political attitudes is present within all levels of the control variable. Thus, *both* among Jews who do not belong to a synagogue and perform none of the listed rituals and among Jews who belong to a synagogue and perform at least five of the six rituals, women are more likely than men to endorse pro-policy items.

We next turn to sociodemographic factors that may account for this difference. Let us first consider education. Because men have on the average a higher education level than women, the observed difference may be due to differences in educational attainment. Table 4.3 presents sex differences in attitudes within levels of education. Again, the overall pattern remains: women offer greater support for current Israeli policy positions than comparably educated men.

Age is another background factor that must be considered. We see in the second panel of table 4.3 that in general age does seem to be directly related to political attitudes. The older the respondent, the more likely that she or he holds pro-Israeli policy attitudes. Because the women in the study are older than the men, the overall sex difference might be an artifact of the age distribution of the sexes. Moreover, we might expect less of a sex difference among the younger age groups because it is likely that the experiences of the sexes over successive cohorts have become more similar in terms of education, work experience, and social experiences in general. The younger groups have also come of age in an era when sex-role egalitarianism has been more stressed. Thus, we would expect these sex differences to be less pronounced in the younger age group. However, when we examine table 4.3 we see that the original sex difference holds within each age group.

TABLE 4.2

Selected Attitudes toward Israel, by Sex, Controlling for Liberalism and Ritual Observance (percentage)

| | Liberalism[a] | | | | | | Ritual Observance[b] | | | | | | | |
| | Low | | Medium | | High | | Secular | | Minimal | | Moderate | | Observant | |
Attitude[c]	M	F	M	F	M	F	M	F	M	F	M	F	M	F
Support Israeli policies[d]	77	89	78	86	51	68	62	84	70	79	79	86	81	87
Return territories to Arab control for peace	37	59	57	48	23	35	23	36	35	62	36	56	43	58
Should not criticize Israel's policies publicly	37	60	36	59	16	29	28	38	29	35	35	51	39	56
Should not vote for candidates unfriendly to Israel	75	91	70	84	58	69	55	68	71	79	77	81	73	96
Median N	(159)	(98)	(118)	(114)	(71)	(78)	(68)	(23)	(142)	(128)	(79)	(84)	(61)	(56)

[a] Based on answers to nine issues: defense spending, abortion, busing, death penalty, affirmative action, ERA, homosexual teachers, immigration laws, social welfare spending, and an item on political self-identification.

[b] Based on synagogue membership and performance of following rituals: attend a Passover seder; light Chanukah candles; regularly light Sabbath candles; fast on Yom Kippur; attend services on Rosh Hashana; different dishes for meat and dairy products.

[c] See table 4.1 for item working and response categories analyzed.

[d] Percentage "about right" or "too dovish."

TABLE 4.3
Selected Attitudes toward Israel, by Sex, Controlling for Education, Age, and Employment (percentage)

| Attitude[a] | Education | | | | | | | | Age | | | | | | Full-Time Employment | | | |
| | HS or less | | Some college | | BA | | MA+ | | 18-39 | | 40-59 | | 60+ | | No | | Yes | |
	M	F	M	F	M	F	M	F	M	F	M	F	M	F	M	F	M	F
Support Israeli policies[b]	78	88	81	90	81	77	62	72	66	76	71	86	79	89	77	83	69	82
Return territories to Arab control for peace	38	53	40	51	42	48	24	42	26	44	42	51	35	53	33	53	34	46
Should not criticize Israel's policies publicly	59	65	43	51	31	44	16	22	19	26	34	51	44	59	41	44	26	37
Should not vote for candidates unfriendly to Israel	73	90	72	86	70	82	67	72	64	76	69	84	77	90	72	87	68	75
Median N	(60)	(60)	(61)	(70)	(88)	(77)	(135)	(76)	(122)	(114)	(105)	(95)	(124)	(81)	(95)	(144)	(221)	(126)

[a] See table 4.1 for item wording and response categories analyzed.
[b] "about right" or "too dovish."

Indeed, the relationship between attitudes and sex seems to be as strong in the youngest age group as in the oldest.

A final sociodemographic variable to be examined is employment status. Again, this factor varies with sex and is expected to be related to political attitudes. Specifically, if women are less involved in the work world outside the home, a greater portion of their identity might rest on Jewish components. They may have less contact with non-Jews, and they may be more traditional in their outlook. Therefore, they might be expected to be more sympathetic to current Israeli policy. The final panel of table 4.3. shows that differences in employment status do not account for the original sex differences. Even among those employed outside the home on a full-time basis, women are more likely to endorse pro-Israeli policy statements.[6]

In sum, in groups in which we would expect this sex difference to disappear (the highly liberal, the nonobservant, the young, the highly educated, full-time participants in the labor force), we *still* find that a higher proportion of women than men profess attitudes that are consistent with current Israeli government policy. We have considered many of the factors that we might have expected to account for the original sex difference and now turn to an explanation that relates to another finding discovered in these data.

The women in this sample were more likely than the men to manifest a fundamental insecurity over the status of American Jewry. Women were less likely than the men to agree that "there is a bright future for Jewish life in America" (66 percent versus 75 percent), and that "virtually all positions of influence in America were open to Jews" (28 percent versus 38 percent). Although almost all respondents personally felt that U.S. support for Israel is in the U.S. interest, women were less likely to agree that "most Americans think that U.S. support for Israel is in America's interest" (27 percent versus 53 percent). Finally, women were also more likely to see anti-Semitism as a "very important" issue confronting American Jews (89 percent versus 79 percent).

Thus, it seems that American Jewish women tend to see the United States as a less hospitable environment for Jewry than do men. This perception may affect their willingness to take a more dovish position regarding Israel's future.[7] The four items discussed above were combined into a single scale. As table 4.4. demonstrates, when we compare men and women within different levels on this scale of perceptions of the United States as a hostile environment, the original pattern of sex differences still holds. The sex differences remain even though women do perceive the environment as more hostile to Jews than do men and even though, as table 4.4 demonstrates, such perceptions are related to the expression of more hawkish views on the Middle East conflict.

TABLE 4.4
Selected Attitudes, by Sex, Controlling for Perceptions of U.S. as Hostile (percentage)

Attitude[a]	Low		Medium		High	
	M	F	M	F	M	F
Support Israeli[b] policies	69	76	73	85	79	85
Return territories for peace	29	34	28	50	53	61
Not criticize	33	38	29	43	36	49
Not vote for unfriendly candidates	63	74	73	84	80	87
Median N	(165)	(91)	(107)	(97)	(75)	(100)

Note: See text for item wording.
[a] See table 4.1 for item wording.
[b] Percentage "about right" or "too dovish."

Our analysis thus far has taken account of relevant control variables that might have explained the pattern of sex differences observed in tables 4.1 through 4.4. Although these control variables, when considered individually, do not account for the sex difference, it might be the case that they do so in combination. The extent of endorsement of the attitudes of interest by sex was unaffected by adjusting, using multiple classification analysis, for the joint effects of all the control variables (age, education, employment, liberalism, perception of United States as hostile, ritual observance) simultaneously.[8] Thus, even when considered together, these variables failed to account for the sex differences in attitudes toward Israel.

Summary and Discussion

We found that sex differences in American Jews' attitudes toward Israel occurred at the level of policy and acts supporting that policy rather than in attitudes of general concern and commitment. This difference was robust enough to withstand successive and joint controls of theoretically relevant variables. American Jewish women, probably because of their high level of concern for Israel, are not as dovish as the general literature on hawkishness/dovishness would lead us to believe. Given the equivalent level of concern on the part of Jewish women and men, might not these differences reflect alternative manifestations of this concern? As Hertzberg (1979; 285) reminds us:

> The difference between doves and hawks in the American Jewish community is not a difference between weak commitment and strong, or even between

bleeding hearts and warmongers. It is an honest difference between people whose fundamental commitment to Israel's safety is equally powerful but who differ, as thoughtful people will, regarding the best way of insuring that security.

Thus, women may differ from men as to their perception of the optimal way of acting on their strong concern for Israel.

The hawk/dove distinction may not be appropriate in this context. For example, Decter (*Public Opinion* 1982b; 20,41) recently argued that women's greater dovish inclinations are part of their preoccupation with preventing "various forms of harm from coming to those they are looking after." The views of American Jewish women on Israeli policy provide an interesting test case buttressing Decter's assertion. Whereas on global issues, this threat may concern the use of force and its catastrophic consequences, it might be that with respect to Israel, the perception of harm concerns a lack of preparedness and the risk of compromising Israel's defense posture. Thus, the same underlying dynamic that predisposes women to be more dovish on global issues may have the opposite effect regarding Israel.

It would be of interest to see if future studies of American Jewish attitudes toward Israel replicate this pattern of results. Furthermore, we need to explore further the basis of this difference. Assuming that men and women have equally high levels of concern about Israel and its survival, what factors account for their differing policy orientations? It is likely that further exploration of this issue will also shed light on possible sex differences in Jewish identity as a whole.

Notes

I thank Steven M. Cohen for making the data available to me and for his valuable comments. Harold Himmelfarb, Charles Liebman, Peter Medding, Lawrence Sternberg, David Varady, and Jonathan Woocher also made helpful comments. An earlier version of this paper was presented at the annual meeting of the North Central Sociological Association, Columbus, Ohio, April 29, 1983.
1. We do not know if such a distinction holds among Jews. Welch and Ullrich (1984) report that due to the relatively high liberalism of Jewish men, Jewish women, unlike their gentile counterparts, are not more likely to oppose military spending. On the other hand, they report that Jewish women are generally the most liberal politically. Unfortunately, they were not able to directly examine attitudes regarding war and military intervention.
2. For an analysis of the merits of this technique, see Himmelfarb et al. (1984).
3. See Cohen (1982) for more detailed information on sampling.
4. Ten of the original 673 respondents did not indicate their sex, and their responses were eliminated.

5. A subsequent national sample conducted in April through August of 1984 contained a similar item, which read: "Israel should offer the Arabs territorial compromise in Judea and Samaria (the West Bank) in return for credible guarantees of peace." The sex differences were of a similar order: 47.1 percent of the men versus 36.6 percent of the women agreed. Such a replication increases our confidence in the validity of the responses in the original sample.
6. Although employment status does not explain away the original sex difference, it is the case that women who are housewives have the highest levels of concern for Israel and support of Israeli policy across nearly *all* items lited in table 4.1. Thus, the exploration of the dynamics of Jewish identity among this group of women deserves special attention.
7. Writing about the relationship between the fundamental insecurity in the Diaspora and Israel as a place of refuge, Hertzberg (1979; 283) notes; "Those who guarantee an 'insurance policy' (in this case the Israelis) assess the risks more or less realistically; the insured, the Amerian Jews, tend to be more worried."
8. Adjusted percentages are available from the author.

References

Argyle, Michael, and Benjamin Beit-Hallahmi. 1975. *The Social Psychology of Religion*. Boston: Routledge & Kegan Paul.
Batson, C. Daniel, and W. Larry Ventis. 1982. *The Religious Experience*. New York: Oxford University Press.
Cohen, Steven M. 1982. "The 1981-1982 National Survey of American Jews." *American Jewish Year Book* 83:89-110.
Frankovic, Kathleen. 1982. "Sex and Politics—New Alignments, Old Issues." *PS* 15:439-48.
Hertzberg, Arthur. 1979. *Being Jewish in America*. New York: Schocken.
Himmelfarb, Harold, R. Michael Loar, and Susan Mott. 1984. "Sampling by Ethnic Surnames: The Case of American Jews." *Public Opinion Quarterly* 47:247-60.
Liebman, Charles. 1973. *The Ambivalent American Jew*. Philadelphia: Jewish Publication Society.
Mueller, John E. 1973. *War, Presidents and Public Opinion*. New York: Wiley.
Public Opinion. 1982a. "Women and Men: Is Realignment Under Way?" 5 (April/May):21-32.
_____. 1982b. "Are Women Different Today?" 5 (April/May):20,41.
Sklare, Marshall, and Joseph Greenblum. 1979. *Jewish Identity on the Suburban Frontier*. 2d ed. Chicago: University of Chicago Press.
Vernon, Glenn, and Jerry Cardwell. 1980. "Males, Females and Religion." In *The Social Context of Religiosity*, ed. Jerry Cardwell. Lanham, Md.: University Press of America.
Welch, Susan, and Fred Ullrich. 1984. *The Political Life of American Jewish Women*. Fresh Meadows, N.Y.: Biblio Press.

5

The Urban Ecology of Jewish Populations: A Comparative Analysis

Vivian Klaff

The spatial distance between populations can be considered an indicator of social distance. The Jews have traditionally been viewed as living in segregated conditions within urban areas. This paper focuses on three issues: (1) the extent to which Jewish groups are residentially segregated; (2) the extent to which Jewish groups are decentralizing; and (3) the implications of alternative patterns of residential distribution for the Jewish group in urban areas. An analysis of the available data points to decentralization at an ever-increasing rate combined with the tendency to relocate in areas that are Jewish in character. Thus, while clustering or residential segregation persists, it continues in diluted form: concentration does not necessarily reflect isolation, and Jews living in what might be termed a Jewish environment are nevertheless exposed to greater physical and cultural contact with other groups.

Introduction

"If you would know what kind of Jew a man is, ask him where he lives; for no simple factor indicates as much about the character of the Jew as the area in which he lives. It is an index not only to his economic status, his occupation, his religion, but to his politics and his outlook on life and the stage in the assimilative process that he has reached" (Wirth 1928, 57-71). This statement was written by the sociologist Louis Wirth in the 1920s. Despite the fact that Wirth often misrepresented the sociological implications of spatial patterns (because of his ideological viewpoint), the issue he raises in this quotation is as important today as it was for Chicago in the early years of the twentieth century.

The research on residential distribution patterns of minority groups is quite extensive, yet there have been few attempts to conduct a comparative cross-cultural investigation of a specific group in order to examine issues related to the urban ecology of minority groups. The Jewish group is generally considered to be an essentially urban population, and study of Jewish populations in different historical and cultural settings can assist us in documenting strategies of environmental adaptation used by a minority group. To examine the shape of Jewish distribution in Western cities, this overview focuses on three issues that appear to be crucial in understanding the urban ecology of Jewish populations:

1. Are Jewish populations residentially segregated or concentrated, and how do Jews differ in their residential distribution patterns from other ethnic groups?
2. Are Jewish populations decentralizing (suburbanizing), and to what extent is there evidence of the reconcentration of Jews in newly settled areas?
3. What are the determinants and the implications of residential segregation patterns for Jewish populations?

Patterns of Residential Segregation

The classical model of Jewish immigrant residential distribution is represented by the ghetto. There are many examples of the Jewish ghetto in Eastern and Central Europe, the term *ghetto* having originated with the creation of a distinct neighborhood as a means of social control over sixteenth-century Venice's Jewish population. These areas of extremely high segregation of Jews from non-Jews represent an important phase in early Jewish urban ecology. As recently as 1971 Johnson, an influential writer in urban sociology, stated, "The Jews are the usually quoted example of a minority group who have chosen to continue to live in ghetto situations" (1971, 273).

The evidence on Jewish residential segregation in twentieth-century Western cities is sketchy, due in part to the scarcity of census data regarding religion and in part to the lack of appropriate statistical techniques to undertake comparative analysis. The data for North American cities suggest that patterns of Jewish segregation have persisted beyond the period of initial immigrant status. In a study of the Jewish immigrant population of Chicago, Wirth wrote, "West of the Chicago River, in the shadow of the crowded central business district, lies a densely populated rectangle of tenements representing the greater part of Chicago's immigrant colonies, among them the ghetto" (1928, 195).

A number of studies in the United States have found that Jews (after the initial settlement period) moved rapidly from the working class to the middle class, but there was less of a trend toward residential integration. Glazer and Moynihan (1963, 143) point out that "Jewish residential concentration is not confined to the immigrant generation or the poor. It is a characteristic of the middle and upper-middle classes and the third generation no less than the second." For example, the Chicago "ghetto" referred to by Wirth (1928) is seen over time to have spread westward in the 1930s, and then we find the Jewish population leapfrogging northward to specific neighborhoods in the mid-twentieth century. Jaret in his study of Jewish residential mobility in Chicago concludes that "among Jews the desire to live in close proximity to group members is still strong. Jews tend to live clustered together in residential areas in much greater density than their percentage of the population" (Jaret 1979, 241). What general evidence is there to support these statements by Glazer and Moynihan, and Jaret?

A series of index of dissimilarity matrixes prepared for Cleveland by Uyeki (1980) for the years 1910 through 1970 show that the average index of segregation of Russians (a predominantly Jewish group) from other European immigrant groups has (with few exceptions in the earlier years) been consistently the highest of all the intergroup averages. Although there are obvious problems with the use of Russian foreign stock census data as a proxy for Jews, due to the aging of the population, the Cleveland data and similar analyses of other U.S. cities confirm continuing segregative tendencies of Jewish groups (Kantrowitz 1979; Guest and Weed 1971; Rees 1979).

In recent years new sources of data have become available for use in analyzing Jewish residential distribution, namely, Jewish community surveys (Tobin and Lipsman 1984). A general review of the data on geographic location in these studies clearly shows that in many cities there are areas with high concentrations of Jewish populations. For example, in Baltimore 85 percent of Jews live in seven zip code zones; in St. Louis 88 percent of Jewish households are found in ten contiguous zip code zones to the west of the downtown area; in the north shore of Milwaukee three zip code zones contain 59 percent of Jewish households; and in Pittsburgh 43 percent of Jewish households are found in Squirrel Hill. These community survey data sets suggest that Jewish populations continue to cluster in varying degrees from city to city.

A problem with these studies is that none compares Jewish location with the location of other religious or ethnic population subgroups. Thus, we need to be careful not to confuse the concentration of Jews in an area (i.e. the percentage of all of the Jews who are resident in an area) with the Jewishness of an area (i.e. the percentage of a city's total Jewish population who are resident in a particular area). In fact, in most areas for which the data point to a concentration of Jewish population, the population is generally a minority in the area. For example, 25 percent of all the Jewish persons in the eight-county New York area live in Brooklyn, but they represent only 19 percent of the population of Brooklyn.

The evidence presented above suggests that Jewish populations, as in the past, continue to be concentrated and tend to be segregated in their residential location from other population subgroups in urban areas. This continued tendency among Jewish populations to maintain some degree of separateness in the context of high mobility and suburbanization calls for future investigation. The question now posed is: Are Jewish populations decentralizing (suburbanizing), and to what extent is there evidence of continued concentration of Jews in newly settled neighborhoods?

Patterns of Ecological Redistribution

The classicial ecological model of social morphology for large industrialized U.S. cities presented by Park and Burgess in the 1920s (Burgess 1925) states that the city center was the watershed for poor immigrants who used the security of dense inner-city neighborhoods close to the economic center of the city as their initial point of settlement. In time these immigrant groups moved out and were replaced by new immigration groups. This model, commonly referred to as the concentric zone model, suggests that the socioeconomic status of the urban population increases as we move from the center of the city to the periphery.

Competing models have been developed that suggest that population and housing characteristics differ according to wedges running from the center to the periphery (for the sector model, see Hoyt 1928), or that several nuclei serve as organizing foci for the city's development, with subgroups arranged according to concentric or sectorial configurations around each nuclei (Harris and Ullman 1945).

Ecological models of residential patterns suggest that immigrant groups initially cluster in ethnic inner-city neighborhoods but eventually are absorbed into the wider society as they spread into peripheral areas. In general in industrialized societies, the twentieth century has seen a phenomenon of decentralization of population, more generally known as suburbanization. These centrifugal movements do not necessarily imply a concomitant breakdown of segregation, for it is possible for segregated patterns to reemerge in new areas. Goldstein (1981) makes the point that Jews in the United States are suburbanizing at a significant rate. Evidence from community studies are generally supportive of this statement. Although a few cities manifest multimodal decentralizing patterns and some evidence suggests that Jews are slower to move out of the city centers than other ethnic groups, the majority of studies conclude that (a) the Jewish population is suburbanizing in a sectorial fashion, and (b) new concentrations develop as the population spreads from the core-city immigrant locations to the suburbs. Illustrations of this phenomenon are found in studies of mobility patterns reported in Cleveland (eastward), St. Louis (westward), Philadelphia (northward), Miami (northeast), Pittsburgh (southeast), Seattle (eastward), and Cincinnati (northward), among others.

A study of Jewish residential mobility in Chicago covering the years 1960 to 1974 (Jaret 1979) reported that the desire by Jews to live in close proximity to group members was still strong. Some specific findings are that Jews have been suburbanizing along with the rest of the population, but the major proportion of moves by Jews can be classified as *within*-city moves, and Jews moving to suburbs tend to be less concentrated in areas, but still concentrated in blocks along certain streets. An analysis of Boston data suggests that in the early decades of the twentieth century the Jewish population was heavily concentrated in the central city (Fowler 1977). By the late 1950s and early 1960s the Jewish population was predominatly dispersed in north and west sections of the city, and by the mid-1970s there had been further decentralization, and large reductions in the number of Jews in Boston had occurred. Little is known, however, of levels of concentration or segregation due to the limited nature of the data.

The most illustrative and comprehensive work on the residential distribution pattern of Jews in North America has been done by various researchers on Toronto, Canada. The Canadian census is one of the few modern censuses that reports population statistics by religion. In addition, the Jewish group is included as one category in the ethnic-origin classification. Toronto is a large heterogeneous city with a substantial Jewish population that in 1961 was estimated at 66,000, approximately 5.4 percent of the metropolitan total. Rosenberg's data from the 1950 census demonstrate that although the Jews were not isolated in a particular neighborhood in the early twentieth century, there was a significant concentration in the inner-city downtown area. By the 1950s the Jewish population had decentralized to quite an extent in a northerly direction (Rosenberg 1954).

The tendency has been toward wider dispersion throughout Toronto as the Jewish population became increasingly integrated in economic and cultural life. As decentralization took place, with Jews moving to the residential suburbs, they still tended to be more centralized than the total population up to 1951, but the 1961 data suggest that Jews were decentralizing at a rapid rate. In 1951 Jews constituted 6.7 percent of Toronto's population and 2.1 percent of the outer suburbs' population; in 1961, 2.8 percent and 7.2 percent. In 1961 less than a tenth of Toronto's Jewish population resided in the traditional reception area for immigrants; about 13 percent lived in Forest Hill village; and more than 50 percent lived in North York township. According to Murdie, the Jews—unlike the

Italians—remained segregated largely by choice so as to be near friends, synagogues, and grocery stores. The Jews have moved northward in sectorial fashion (Murdie 1969, 94-102).

An ongoing geostatistical analysis of Toronto data (Bachi and Klaff 1981) confirms the clustering of Jewish population in the area leading from the northern part of the central city into the northern suburbs, and preliminary analysis of data from the 1971 and 1981 census points to a continuation of the decentralization but a clustering trend in a sectorial northerly direction.

An important issue related to this changing distribution pattern of Jews concerns the characteristics of the neighborhoods as the population decentralizes. Jewish communal leaders are concerned about the increasing decentralization for a number of reasons. A major concern centers on the fact that lesser densities strain organizational abilities to maintain viable religious and communal facilities and increase the expense of doing so. Not only are more and more Jews living farther away from the major Jewish institutions of the community but, evidence shows, neighborhoods with significant Jewish populations also tend to differ in demographic characteristics. Areas differ by age structure (in Milwaukee, for example, it was estimated that 24 percent of Jews in the city were sixty-five years or more, compared to 14.3 percent in the North Shore area); by household type (suburban areas tend to have higher percentages of families with young children); and by religious denomination (cities with higher percentages of Orthodox Jews tend to have a greater proportion of the Jewish population closer to the communal institutions). The analysis of these differences and implications for planning decisions to be implemented by local communities should be a notable area of future research.

A final word of caution needs to be issued here concerning the impact of recent migration of a group into an area. It is important to be able to differentiate between decentralization of a Jewish population and the settlement of Jewish immigrants in peripheral areas. We need to be aware that period of immigration may have significant impact on the residential distribution pattern of immigrant groups. Decentralization must not be confused with settlement patterns of groups that arrive at different points in time. New groups may settle in peripheral areas, thus giving the impression of decentralization.

In summary, the evidence suggests that (a) Jewish populations are decentralizing in urban areas with expanding suburbs, but at a slower rate than the general population; (b) moves tend to be sectorial in form; and (c) the Jewish populations are regrouping in new areas or neighborhoods, where new concentrations of Jewish populations are found. Having pointed out the extent and nature of Jewish residential distribution patterns, we now turn to the question of why these patterns exist and some implications of these patterns. This is obviously a large task, but a start will be made by reviewing settlement ideologies as they affect populations and the consequences of residential differentiation.

Determinants and Implications of Residential Segregation

Explanations of the concentration of Jews include institutional barriers in the housing market, specific socioeconomic status characteristics of the Jewish population, and Jews' voluntary desire to live in close proximity to other Jews and to Jewish institutions. The residential clustering of population subgroups is neither a random nor a nonrational process. Although the classical ecological approach to explaining location decisions is based on the outcome of economic competition for space and the trade-off between time and space, it is evident that we cannot ignore the importance of values and the many other influences, subjective and objective, on decision making. Of particular importance is an understanding of settlement ideologies. Both the receiving host society and a particular minority group generally have a perspective on the process of interaction in the society and on their ideological commitment to this model of interaction.

The vast majority of writings about the impact of residential distribution of racial, ethnic, or other minority groups on social integration use the assimilationist model, which suggests that (a) residential isolation is an important indicator of the lack of assimilation, and (b) minority groups desire assimilation into the mainstream culture of the society (Hawley and Rock 1973). Researchers have maintained that the degree of residential segregation is an acceptable indicator of, or a proxy for, assimilation. An ethnically enclosed residential experience insulates a group from important mechanisms of assimilation, limits cross-cultural contacts that affect the socialization of the young, and has serious implications for subsequent experiences such as intermarriage, upward job mobility, and the formation of social ties. Specifically, it is suggested that segregation resists social mobility and has particularly negative effects on the psychological development of the group that is segregated. Thus, the lower the degree of segregation, the greater the likelihood that a goup is experiencing assimilation. Desegregation, then, is likely to result in a dissipation of the subordinate status, and hence the assimilation of the subjugated group into the mainstream society (Marston and Van Valey 1979).

Investigation of societies with ethnic minorities reveals that residential segregation persists in most of them, and in many situations ethnic group identity has persisted and become more salient (Glazer and Moynihan 1970; Newman 1973). This represents a different model, leading to alternative forms of social interaction. In some societies the trend is toward preservation of elements of culture within the national unity of the society. It is suggested that residential segregation is an important element in the maintenance of this pluralist model of integration in that ethnic residential clusters in cities perform certain positive functions.

The discussion of the pluralist model in the general ecological literature is complex, for it is difficult, with available data, to dissaggregate the contributions to segregative tendencies of voluntary forces from those of involuntary forces (Greeley 1974; Metzger 1971). In most situations discrimination and voluntary self-segregation may be opposite sides of the same coin. Where the host society controls the housing market either overtly by means of segregative settlement policy (e.g. Jews allowed to live only in a certain area) or covertly by means of institutional barriers (e.g. loans not available to Jews), the consequences are high levels of involuntary separation. It is generally considered that barriers to open housing have decreased as a factor in Jewish residential location and that other factors have assumed greater importance.

One important factor concerns the part that economic status plays in the distribution of ethnic groups. Generally the research findings in the United States suggest that the higher the occupational status of the group, the less residentially segregated it is from native-born whites of native parents. The question of whether ethnic groups are residentially segregated because of their ethnicity (ethnic status model) or socioeconomic status (class model) is an important research issue (Guest and Weed 1971). Studies of social stratification in North America have found that Jews moved at rapid rates from working class to middle class. An associated finding was that Jewish residential concentration was not confined to the immigrant generation or the poor. The pattern of concentration was found to be characteristic of the middle and upper classes, and the third generation no less than the second generation.

Summary data presented by Rees point out that in U.S. cities a major exception to the residence-status relationship is "the Russian group." The Russians are the group with the highest educational and occupational status, and yet they are the least residentially assimilated of the European ethnic groups. "A very strong preference for living in a Jewish community among coethnics together with some degree of housing discrimination against Jews in the past undoubtedly account for the residential concentration of the Russian foreign stock group in all the urbanized areas . . ." (Rees 1979; 327, 330). Concluding their analysis of the ethnic differences in the residential search process in Toronto, Gad et al. state: "The Jews, more than Italians, form a close-knit community with strong social, cultural and economic ties, and are motivated to maintain these ties. They are also aware of the location of social contacts and Jewish institutions and take these into consideration in a relocation decision (1973;179). In general, however, very little empirical information is available concerning differential residential distribution of socioeconomic subgroups of ethnic population within cities. A comprehensive review of the determinants of the distribution patterns and functions, both positive and negative, for the Jewish group is crucial to our understanding of the urban ecology of minority groups, and should be seen as an impotant area of future research.

Conclusion

Although the research on residential distribution patterns of minority groups is extensive, there have been few attempts to conduct a comparative cross-cultural investigation of a specific group in order to examine issues related to the urban ecology of minority groups. The Jewish group is generally considered to be an essentially urban population, and study of Jewish populations in different historical and cultural settings can assist us in examining strategies of environmental adaptation used by a minority group. The perspective of urban ecology has made it possible to draw certain conclusions about the historical development of Jewish populations in urban settings. Although many of the data are not current and do not bring us completely up to date, nevertheless it has been possible to make summary statements about the residential structure of Jewish communities.

The overall summary statement that seems most applicable from the review of information points to the Jewish trend of decentralization at an ever-increasing rate combined with the tendency to relocate in areas that are Jewish in character. Thus, although clustering, or residential segregation persists, it is diluted; concentration does not necessarily reflect isolation, and Jews living in what might be termed a Jewish environment in the suburbs are nevertheless exposed to greater physical and cultural contact with other groups.

The issue of the consequences of residential distribution patterns is highly complex, for it involves subjective perceptions of the meaning of territory. It is, however, important for groups or community leaders to understand the dynamics of settlement patterns. Jewish communal planners whose declared objective is the strengthening of the Jewish community in all aspects appear to have recognized that current mobility patterns will contribute in no small way to the eventual assimilation of increasing numbers of Jews through intermarriage, nonaffiliation with Jewish institutions, and the acceptance of largely secular value systems. A number of strategies seem appropriate in response to the assimilation trend. On the one hand, a group may view increased spatial redistribution of its members as a successful process of integration. Other people may see the need for a critical mass of group membership to maintain viable communal and religious facilities, and they have begun to develop strategies to cope with residential dispersion.

It has been suggested by some observers of the urban scene that a combination of highly personal mobility and modern communication techniques has rendered the notion of territorial constraints on human association obsolescent. To proponents of this view, the concept of community itself becomes devoid of territorial content. To ecologists and geographers, on the other hand, location remains a major determinant of interaction patterns, and the concept of community is firmly anchored on a territorial base. Developments in transportation and communications technology may have lessened territorial constraints, but place of residence is a major factor in allocating life chances and determining interaction patterns. The whole notion of a territorial base to services (local and other) ensures that locality will continue to be of vital importance in the organization of society.

References

Bachi, R., and V. Klaff. 1981. "L'Ecologie urbaine des sous-populations," Compte rendu du colloque *Demographie et destin des sous-populations.* Liège: Association Internationale des Demographes de Langue Française.

Burgess, W. 1925. "The Growth of the City: An Introduction to a Research Project." In *The City,* ed. R.E. Park, E.W. Burgess, and R.D. McKenzie. Chicago: University of Chicago Press.

Darrock, A.G., and W.G. Marston. 1971. "The Social Class Basis of Ethnic Residential Segregation: The Canadian Case." *American Journal of Sociology* 491-510.

Fowler, F.J. 1977. *A Study of the Jewish Population of Greater Boston.* Boston: Combined Jewish Philanthropies of Greater Boston.

Gad, G., R. Peddie, and J. Punter. 1973. "Ethnic Differences in the Residential Search Process." In *The Form of Cities in Central Canada: Selected Papers,* ed. L.S. Bourne, R.D. MacKinnon, and J.W. Simmons, pp. 168-180. Toronto: University of Toronto.

Glazer, N., and D.P. Moynihan. 1970/1963. *Beyond the Melting Pot.* Cambridge: MIT Press.

Goldstein, S. 1981. "Jews in the United States: Perspectives from Demography." In *American Jewish Yearbook* 81:3-59.

Greeley, A. 1974. *The Demography of Ethnic Identification.* Chicago: Center for the Study of American Pluralism, University of Chicago.

Guest, A.M., and J.A. Weed. 1971. "Ethnic Residential Segregation: Patterns of Change." *American Journal of Sociology* 81:1088-1111.

Harris, C., and E. Ullman. 1945. "The Nature of Cities." *Annals of the American Academy of Political and Social Science* 242:7-17.

Hawley, A.H., and V.P. Rock, eds. 1973. *Segregation in Residential Areas.* Washington: National Academy of Sciences.

Hoyt, H. 1928. *The Structure and Growth of Residential Neighborhoods in American Cities.* Washington, D.C.: Government Printing Office.

Jaret, C. 1979. "Recent Patterns of Chicago Jewish Residential Mobility." *Ethnicity* 6:235-48.

Johnson, R.J. 1971. *Urban Residential Patterns.* London: Bell & Sons.

Kantrowitz, N. 1979. "Racial and Ethnic Residential Segregation: Boston 1830-1970." *Annals of the American Academy of Political and Social Science* 441:41-54.

Marston, W.G., and T.L. Van Valey. 1979. "The Rise of Residential Segregation in the Assimilation Process." *Annals of the American Academy of Political and Social Science* 441:13-25.

Metzger, L.P. 1971. "American Sociology and Black Assimilation: Conflicting Perspectives." *American Journal of Sociology* 76(4):627-45.

Murdie, R.A. 1969. *Factorial Ecology of Metropolitan Toronto, 1951-1961.* Research Paper No. 116. Chicago: Department of Geography, University of Chicago.

Newman, W.M. 1973. *American Pluralism: A Study in Minority Groups and Social Theory.* New York: Harper & Row.

Rees, P.H. 1979. *Residential Patterns in American Cities: 1960.* Research Paper No. 189. Chicago: Department of Geography, University of Chicago.

Rosenberg, L. 1954. *The Changes in the Geographic Distribution of the Jewish Population in the Metropolitan Area of Toronto, 1851-1951.* Toronto: Canadian Jewish Population Studies, Jewish Community Series No. 2.

Tobin, G.A., and J.A. Lipsman. 1984. "A Compendium of Jewish Demographic Studies." In *Perspectives in Jewish Population Research*, ed. S.M. Cohen, J.S. Woocher, and B.A. Phillips, pp. 137-66. Boulder, Colo.: Westview Press.

Uyeki, E.S. 1980. "Ethnic and Race Segregation, 1910-1970." *Ethnicity* 7:390-403.

Wirth, L. 1928. *The Ghetto.* Chicago: University of Chicago Press.

DIALOGUE AND DEBATE

The purpose of this section is to provide a forum for dialogue and debate about a theoretical or methodological concern. We initiated this section in Volume 7 (the First Annual) by focusing on a methodological issue, the use of "distinctive Jewish names" (DJN) as a basis for conducting sample surveys in the Jewish community. In this volume we turn our attention to a discussion of the linkages between theoretical understanding of social life and the social scientific study of Jewry, a topic too often ignored. We asked Samuel Z. Klausner, a former editor of Contemporary Jewry *and a former president of the Association, to write the lead essay in this section. His essay, "What Is Conceptually Special about a Sociology of Jewry," concerns a topic about which he had spoken at a conference several years ago at the University of Connecticut.*

Several scholars were asked to comment on Klausner's essay on the basis of their own theoretical and empirical interests. Responses were received from Calvin Goldscheider, J. Alan Winter, and Walter P. Zenner. They represent the diverse perspectives of research orientations from the fields of demography, sociology of religion, and anthropology, respectively. Although there is no uniformity of opinion about specifics, there is a common theme present in their writings about the desirability of a closer linkage of the empirical study of Jewry with a theoretical understanding of human behavior for the enhancement and enrichment of the perspective of both the particular and universal phenomena. This dialogue and debate will be most productive if it stimulates social scientists to bridge the gap between theory and research. Additional comments from readers to continue this dialogue are welcome and will be considered for publication in future volumes.

6

What Is Conceptually Special about a Sociology of Jewry

Samuel Z. Klausner

The sociology of Jewry specifies general sociological concepts for its particular subject matter. It also offers general sociology new concepts developed in the study of Jewry for application to other areas of study. Though a discipline is not defined by what it studies but by how it studies, it is necessary to define an object of study for a sociology of Jewry. The definition of Jewry might be in terms of the expectations of action in concert, a rule referring to acting rather than being Jewish. This rule also leads to an image of several Jewries. Periodization of the history of these Jewries should follow the unfolding of events internal to each Jewry. Rules for measurement of religiousness or commitment would take the cultural distinctions among these Jewries into consideration. The sociology of Jewry needs to promote its intellectual ties with the humanistic study of Jewry, especially if its practitioners aim to contribute to Jewish social policy.

The Applied Sociology of Jewry

The sociology of Jewry is an applied, not a theoretical or general, sociology. The general concepts of scientific sociology, which may be used to describe *any* human society, are used to classify the behavior of Jews and Jewry. The concept of *stratification*, for example, refers to any hierarchy of social authority. Applied to economic relations, for instance, it refers to the subordination of feudal serfs to their lords, and with equal validity to distinctions among capitalist economic classes. The general idea of stratification is tailored, or "specified," for each particular setting. Aristotle, in *Politics*, distinguished the way fathers dominate sons from the way governors dominate citizens. The specification of the general idea of dominance permits us to speak of what distinguishes these two relations in the light of

73

that which they share. The sociology of Jewry specifies such general concepts for the study of Jews and Jewish society.[1]

The manner of this specification reveals what is conceptually special about a sociology of Jewry. At the same time a sociology of Jewry develops its own concepts through experience with its own subject matter. These may become general concepts and subsequently be specified for other fields.

This paper comments on five selected methodological issues in the sociology of Jewry: (1) the matter of conceptual specification; (2) the definition of the field; (3) the measurement of religious Jewishness; (4) the periodization of Jewish history; and (5) the relation of the sociology of Jewry to the humanistic study of Judaism. By deriving rules for conceptual specification, we provide a frame for defining the field. The field definition is not the initial source of conceptual rules in an empirical discipline, as it might be in rational philosophical discourse. Our opening topic, therefore, is that of conceptual specification.

Concepts Are Rules for Seeing

Concepts are rules for seeing. The rules are modified to fit what we want to see. They draw attention to abstracted attributes of social events. The concrete events provide empirical guidance about sensible ways of abstracting from them.

General sociological concepts are, themselves, developed in a particular empirical context. To stay with our example, the idea of stratification crystallized in studies of polities. The stratification metaphor, borrowed from geology, enhances our vision of the unseen polity. It also distorts the reality of the polity in its emphasis on hierarchy and, perhaps, the fixedness of hierarchy among all of the power struggle processes that characterize political relations. The metaphor also distorts our vision because social dominance is not as neatly and carefully layered as are the walls of the Grand Canyon. The functional division of labor, which characterizes the polity, arranges its segments differently than does erosion and sedimentation. The latter know nothing, for instance, about "organic solidarity."

To speak of stratification within the family is to build a metaphor on a metaphor. The idea of patriarchy, for example, is the specification of the idea of stratification for kinship relations. A disadvantage of this application of the general to the specific is that the concept of stratification induces us to think politically about primary relationships. Yet, we know that the affective and diffuse character, to use Parsons's terms, of familial relations limits the instrumental exertion of political power in the family. The advantage of applying such a general concept, of treating patriarchy as a special case of stratification, is that it establishes the basis for a comparative sociology, a comparison of hierarchization in several institutions.

The specification of general sociological concepts for the sociology of Jewry traverses several steps. First, the concepts of organization and leadership are developed in political and industrial studies. Transferred to the sociology of religion, they become religious organization and religious leadership. Aspects of *Gemeinschaft* and of charisma modify the original instrumental imagery. Second, these latter concepts have been used, primarily, to describe Christian church organization and leadership. Applying them to synagogue organization and rabbinical roles is a further specification with, yet, a further distortion.

The peculiar lineage of such sociologial concepts defines the Jewish community by social forms it shares with other communities, first, with economic and political life, and second, with Christianity. Jewry is, implicitly, contrasted with these other groups along the shared dimension of, in this instance, organization and leadership. Jewry is characterized as differing in its *value*, or measure, from Christianity on the shared variable. Thus, students of Jewry observe that hierocratic or religious authority is less centralized in Judaism than it is in Catholicism. It may be, though, that Jewish organizational form differs in its pattern from the Christian. A covenantal authority, rooted in Torah and its exegetes, differs from leadership by an apostolic successor directed by the Divine Spirit. Synagogues are not sacramental churches representing the Divine vice-regent, and rabbis, in verbally sacralizing a meal, are not priests participating in a transubstantiation of material to spiritual reality.

Sociological concepts, on the whole, are intellectual tools of the Western academic mind—more particularly, of European rationalism. Sociology's major traditions were forged in the hearth of Western industrialism. Marx's categories, as one example of Western thought, such as the modes of production and their internal contradictions or the tension between authorized and alienated labor, relegate the categories of Jewry's self-standing to mere epiphenomena.

The sacralization of the world, the permanent authority of the covenant, and *avodah* as sacred labor appear to Marx as elements in a false consciousness surviving vestigially on sufferance, relics of a long-deceased mode of production. It may even be empirically demonstrable that crucial elements of the ideas crystallized in a priestly Judean jurisdiction under Persian suzerainty. A categorization of Jewish ideas as vestigial is consistent with the observed deterioration of Jewish consciousness in capitalist, and socialist, societies and is, therefore, certainly a seductive intellectual apparatus. Marxian sociology in its orthodox forms, falters as an explanatory framework for Jewry. The strength and quality of adherence to the covenant, for instance, seem unrelated to the strength of class consciousness, and have been reincarnated in the sequence of noncapitalist Jewish societies from the premonarchic tribal period to the present. The Marxian framework becomes increasingly telling for the study of Jewry as that community becomes part of the modern capitalist world in the United States and in Israel, for example.

A sociological frame of reference, whether Marxian, Weberian, Parsonian, or of the Chicago school, reconstructs the behavioral reality of its subjects in its own rationalistic schema. Sociology's reconstruction of Jewry reinterprets the reality of quotidian Jews as they live it. This reconstruction distorts reality less if the general sociological terms are domesticated for Jewish life. Jewish particularity is not to be dismissed nor the essentially Jewish obscured by general concepts. To fail to tailor the general concept is, at worst, reductionist. The Jewish becomes simply a variant on Western-Christian experience. At best, the fixation on commonality promoted by unspecified general concepts obscures the *differentia specifica*, the uniqueness of Jewry.

There is a practical, empirical side to this. General concepts imposed on ill-fitting data lead to statistically insignificant correlations. In all research the initial general concept is tendered as a vague approximation to an intended data classification, in Paul Lazarsfeld's words, "some vaguely conceived entity that makes the observed relations meaningful." When general sociological concepts are used to ask questions of Jewish experience, that experience may protest the question or may provide a Jewish answer. The outcome is a specification, a clearer definition of the original concept, tailored for the Jewish material.

The uniqueness of Jewry is crystallized in Jewish cultural values. Humanistic students of Jewish culture identify the uniquely Jewish by interpreting the written repositories of Jewry and Judaism. The ideas and values they discover are definitively Jewish even when traceable to Akkadian or Islamic sources. The reason for this is that the immigrant ideas have entered synergistically into a social system understood as Jewish. When, however, humanistic scholars transcend the text, say with literary criticism, they embed the text within a matrix of foreign concepts. The Jewish *haskalah* scholars writing Hebrew fiction and the German students of *Wissenschaft des Judentums* did this and admitted to this embedding of Jewish ideas in Western culture. The scholars of the *yeshivot* criticized them for thinking of Judaism in non-Jewish categories. These Jewish humanists, for much the same reasons that we offer, accepted sociological concepts as adequate for studying Jewry. They expand the power of our analysis (and, of course, integrate us within a community of scholars).

Today's sociologists of Jewry rarely ask a Jewish question, that is, one framed by ideas formed in Jewish experience. Yet, a Jewish sociological idea is not impossible. The sociologist may, following the humanists, take the formal ideas of the literary heritage as a point of reference, but then adapt these ideas to the actual formulations of particular Jewish communities. The Judaic notions of purity or of covenant lead to distinctly Judaic ways of thinking about belongingness, identity, and obligation. The meanings of these terms vary with the particular time and community to which they are applied. They are a frame for empirical studies of today's, and yesterday's, Jews, forming the actual objects and events that Jews avoid and seek, approve and disapprove, love and hate.

Jewish ideas to *describe* Jewry also *interpret* Jewry. Ideas shape a fact and pattern a congeries of facts. In scientific sociology the patterning is of external attributes of behavioral phenomena, called by earlier philosophers secondary qualities.

The knowledge produced by attention to such attributes is perspectival. For example, the idea of the size of a population, whether the Jewish or the Chinese population, refers to an enumeration of objects, here people, within a spatial bound. The enumeration abstracts the fact of physical presence, or absence, from all the other characteristics of the people. Similarly, the term *Jewish identification* abstracts the element of symbolic meaning from the wider situation of social action. The idea of identification merges a symbol of group life with the idea of personality. The remainder of the personal and social reality, such as the characteristic of passivity or activity or the division of resources among persons, is set aside. Such abstract concepts are linked in propositions that, in turn, are woven into social theories. A scientific theory constructed in this way is what we think of as positivistic. The unique, if it exists, is, as noted above, in the particular value on the common variable. In this framework the Jewish question becomes whether the intensity of Jewish identification is stronger or weaker than that of Basque or Gypsy identification.

To know a social group truly, in the real world, requires knowing the internal relations among its ideas, actions, and actors. Knowledge of the set of groups to which the group in question belongs, that is, the classification by external attributes, is but one aspect of the group's characterization. Idealist theorists concentrated on the unique configurations of social and cultural elements that constitute the "visible" group. The internally integrative principle for configuring these elements was termed by Weber a *cultural value*. Cognitive cultural values, ideas, are principles of order that prepare the experienced group for scholarly contemplation. Moral cultural values designate a purposeful order. For actors in that social order, they point a direction for action. Ideas such as *the people of Israel* or *chosen us from among all the peoples* are organizing, even mobilizing, cultural values. They both organize thought cognitively and point to what a Jew ought to do morally. The uniquely Jewish is in the configuration and it is in the purposeful process of social action.

The factual and the moral are connected empirically. Factually described events are evaluated by members of a society in light of their theological and philosophical thought. The literary heritage of ideologies and philosophies may formalize the institutionalized values of an age and serve as points of reference for everyday behavior, particularly the behavior of leaders. Operative Jewish ethical judgments, Jewish moral values, taking note of the heritage, approximate consensual agreement among Jews or among Jewish leaders. They may be identified with a consensus among rabbis regarding tradition. Positivistic social theory describes these factual and moral elements from an objective externalist vantage. A *verstehende* analysis, in contrast, draws the analyst into the action, animating the society in its own unique way. Today we tend to walk off stage after completing our description and analysis of attributes, the positivist part of the task. We forget Weber's dictum that causal analysis is a preparation for a meaning, a *verstehende* analysis. The Jewish *verstehende* analysis requires Jewish values, Jewish principles of order guiding the observed social relations.

Now for the caveat. Despite the need to look from within in order to understand life from the vantage of the subject, the scholarly moral duty of the sociologist, any sociologist, is to struggle against the influence of his or her personal values in articulating someone else's social reality. Some sociological work on Jewry, consistent with this norm, has been objective and analytic. Yet, the effort to comprehend the subject's meanings involves seductive closeness to the subject. Ethical interpretations, *cum* ethical proposals, become nearly irresistible. Some of our work, driven by a passion for certain models of Jewish living, has been hortatory. This is a proper role for the ideological leader.

We have spoken of the specification of general concepts for the study of Jewry. A good sociology of Jewry will, in return, contribute to general sociology. Evoking Jewish ideas from Jewish social action can be a basis for new general concepts for studying other societies. The idea of covenanting, for example, is helpful in understanding Puritanism, especially because Puritans drew the term from "Old" Testament texts. As a general sociological concept, covenant could even be used as a model for some non-sacred social relations, a metaphor with Jewish roots for what Durkheim called the "non-contractual elements in contract."

We become aware that we have achieved a mature sociology of Jewry when scholars not otherwise concerned with Jewry study Jews as part of a strategy for elaborating general sociological concerns, when reports of research on Jews appear in general sociological journals and when general sociologists read *Contemporary Jewry* for its contributions to their fields of sociological inquiry.

Defining the Field

A discipline is not defined by what it studies but by how it studies. Sociology is not defined simply as the field that studies society but as the field that uses sociological concepts to study society. Similarly, the sociology of Jewry is not defined simply by the contemplation of Jews as objects but by the use of concepts that formulate, that construct, a Jewish society for analysis. For this reason, this section on the definition of the field had to follow our discussion about the construction of a Jewish social reality.

Although the discipline is defined by its conceptual apparatus, it cannot avoid the polemic about its proper object of study. The construction of Jewry by the sociologist follows its construction by Jews. We do not begin with the individual's feeling of commitment to the group but with the group's expectation. The sociological study of Jewry takes the social collective, not the individual, as its immediate unit of analysis. Jewry is that social group in which members share an expectation of action in concert in support of what are considered to be Jewish values. The group is the constant. The culture is a variable element. The group, in fact, decides upon how variable the culture may be in establishing the boundary between Jew and non-Jew.

Whether an overall world community of Jewry, potential responders to a messianic *kibbutz galuyot*, exists is a question that might be answered empirically. A plurality of Jewries if not one Jewry is discernible by the above definition. Members of a Jewish nation in European Russia are one such Jewry. The American Reform community constitutes another. The *haredim*, strictly Orthodox residents in Israel, Canada, and several other locales, are still another. These Jewries may be loosely confederated.

Slicing the social system in another direction, we may identify Jewish institutions within a larger Jewish polity. Distinct Jewish movements, each with its own identity and values, appear around the institutions. The religion of Judaism, Jewish nationalism, and Jewish agrarianism designate ideologies and systems of action. Each of these social movements may be considered as a member of a larger array of religions, nationalisms, and agrarian political economies subject to study through general sociological concepts. Specification of the Judaic element in each movement illuminates the Jewish case. Thus, Zionism is a particular manifestation of European nationalism, amalgamated with Jewish messianism.

The turn-of-the-century Jewish "religion of labor" is a special case of return-to-nature ideologies, such as those of Tolstoyan peasants or the German *Volk*. The Jewish version is undergirded by a secularized myth of the Abrahamic covenantal promise of a particular land. The configuration of Jewish religion, nationalism, and agrarian political economy, among other organizational entities, constitutes the unique society called Jewry.

Whether this society of Jews is a nation, a nationality, a people, a religious civilization are questions of classification advanced by essayists and theologians for ideological rather than social scientific purposes. Jews' acceptance of one or the other of these ideologies influences their orientation to one another and to the boundaries of Jewish society.

The expectations of action in concert define the boundaries of the Jewries. Popular definitions of the collective boundary do not always correspond to the boundary as officially defined, the legal question of "who is a Jew." For Jews of European Russia, lineage, language, and documentary identification loom large. Ritual circumcision is losing its value as a physical sign of belonging. For the *haredim*, the maternal lineage is crucial, followed by ritual behavioral indicators. An uncircumcised male among them would, to say the least, be ritually defective. The operative norms of the several Jewries are related to the formal definitions in Jewish sacred literature in the way that any actual social norms are related to the formalized legal code of the society.

The actual and the ideal are always in tension and the resolutions of that tension betray the direction of social change. Group boundaries and, implicitly, the designation of members are drawn by the group itself. It is the task of the sociologist to uncover the operative boundary definitions, not to impose them. Occupants of an "ascribed" Jewish status may, in empirical work, be identified by their self-declaration. This declaration must be confirmed by the society of Jewry responsible for the ascription. Simple reliance on individual declarations imprisons the analysis in the subjectivity of the actors. Social science becomes a systematizing of personal ideologies. Discrepancies between the group's assignment, whether by popular norms or by legal formulas, and the actor's declaration may open the way to a study of Jewish false consciousness.

The actor's subjectivity itself becomes an object of analysis for a social psychology of Jewry. Some participate in the life of the collective though not formally qualifying for membership. Contemporary Karaites and Falashas are examples. Some nonparticipants in Jewry nevertheless qualify halakhically, under Talmudic law, as Jews by a rule of descent. They might not be included empirically because they might not meet the requirement of potentially acting in concert as Jews. Highly assimilated children of a Jewishly identifying mother may for all practical purposes have no Jewish ties. Others may meet the requirement of descent but be set aside by the official community for the sin of *avodah zarah*, the worship of false gods. Leaders of non-Jewish religious sects such as Zen Buddhism or the Jews for Jesus, despite apostasy in official Jewish eyes, may still consider themselves to be Jews.

Sometimes the larger non-Jewish society also confirms the ascription but this is not a necessary requirement. The role of external confirmation depends on the sovereignty of the group. American society may punish a draft evader precisely because it does not recognize the legitimacy of his ascribed religious status and does not accept his act as a conscientious objection. American "religious" groups are not sovereign. This is the sense in which Eichmann, or any Nazi leader, would decide who was a Jew.

The previous section opened the question as to what is uniquely Jewish. Jewish cultural values were treated as determinative. Our gloss on this was that the value is defined as Jewish if it is integrated into the social relations of a group understood as Jewish. The previous paragraph defines the boundaries of Jewry in social relational terms. Official Jewry's own self-definition treats culture (sometimes biology) as prior to social relations as the *definiens* of Jewish life. The centrality of Torah is, from this perspective, the foundation for the centrality of peoplehood.

The traditional legal definition, being a child of a Jewish mother, identifies culture with genetics, a Jewish variant on "natural law." *Being* is taken as prior to *acting* as a criterion for inclusion. The "Jew in the street" treats the social as inherited being or inherited cultural traits. Jewry becomes a mystic fraternity.

Why does the social scientist resist accepting this priority of culture over society? For one thing, this approach does not account for the persistence of the group through periods of cultural discontinuity. It flies in the face of Jewry's own historical sense. Further, for the analyst, Christianity, particularly pre-Nicene Christianity, joins Rabbinic Judaism in claiming cultural descent from the cult around the Temple. Jewry adapted to the loss of sovereignty with a continuing intellectual, and worshipful, contemplation of the earlier age. The emerging Christian leadership incorporated some transubstantiated forms of the Temple cult in the mass. The ideologist may decide upon the truth of these claims. The social scientist must take them as data.

For the sociologist, *acting* Jewish (or orienting to acting Jewish) takes precedence over *being* Jewish.[2] Genetic continuity tends to become fictive when one goes beyond immediate generational succession. That contemporary East European Jews are the matrilineal descendants of the conquerors of Canaan is objectively fictive. The fiction is sociologically relevant if current actors orient themselves to it for their self-understanding. The Davidic genealogy offered to legitimate Jesus of Nazareth and the Abrahamic genealogy revitalized to legitimate Islam are, along with the Jewish genealogy, ideological claims. Ideology is a subject of sociological analysis. The behavior of Jews and Jewry may encompass Jewishly relevant activities. These may be the activities of non-Jewish groups, conducted with reference to Jews or having an impact, perhaps unintended, on Jews. In this sense, the study of the Hungarian Iron Guard is relevant to understanding the Holocaust, and the socialization of the Soviet economy during the 1920s is a subject for sociologists of Jewry because it influenced the fate of the Jewish middle classes in the several Soviet republics. Ultimately, the broad concern encompasses the narrow one. The Russian Jewish bourgeoisie and the Soviet policymakers are role partners, complementary actors. Their behaviors are interdependent.

Any definition of Jewry also defines non-Jewry. To define *non-Jews* as a residual, as the logic of the term might suggest, as everybody else in the world, is meaningless. Non-Jews must take Jews into account in their social actions. Christians, members of anti-Semitic movements, and Marranos meet this criterion. The Hindus of Sri Lanka or the Maori of New Zealand are not meaningfully non-Jewish. Non-Jews are the role partners of Jews.

The Measure of Religious Jewishness

Mordecai Kaplan was, of course, correct in describing Judaism, or as we might prefer, Jewry, as a civilization. Until recently, Judaism was not, if it is today, structurally separate from other Jewish institutions. The distinctive religious life of certain Reform circles and the Jewish secular movements have existed for only about a century for any significant number of Jews. Nevertheless, those moments of, as Rudolf Otto put it, awe before the *mysterium tremendum* still permeate Jewish communal and cultural life.

Christians, more than others, have learned to circumscribe the moments of awe institutionally. Secularization circumscribes religiousness (this term sounds better than religiosity) as a personal commitment to specifically religious institutions.

Religiousness itself may be further divided into its components—ritualistic, mystic, experiential, intellectual, and so forth—and personal commitment to each component separately assessed. Although religious commitment is formulated in cosmic terms, sociologists and psychologists studying Christianity assess its mundane reflection. A cultural proxy, assent to a religious dogma, and a social proxy, extent of participation in religious activities, have become common indicators of commitment.

Typically, following William James and Gordon Allport, religiousness is treated as a social psychological concept, the strength or pervasiveness of the bond between the individual and the religious culture or society. The sociological question about the extent of communal mobilization around religious symbols, a question we are now asking about Shi 'ism in Iran, appears less often in the pages of our professional journals.

The religiousness of the collective may ultimately be of more interest to scholars of Jewry than the religiousness of the individual. Many Jewish religious acts involve more than one actor: the *mezuman* of three for concluding a meal, or the *minyan* of ten for reciting kaddish, or the condition that coerced *avodah zarah* be public to establish the expectation of martyrdom. The importance of the religiousness of the collective notwithstanding, this short note will be restricted to the social psychological concept of religiousness.

Sociologists of Jewry encounter problems peculiar to Jewish religiousness. A tolerant ideology in the Western Diaspora allows many ways to be a *good* Jew. Social scientists of Jewry, dutifully following this ideology, have developed measures for each of these types of Jewishness, ethnic and nationalist commitments standing alongside commitment to a life according to halakhah. A galaxy of scales of religiousness based on church attendance and belief has been used for measuring religious Jewishness. Sociologists of Jewry add measures of practical observance of *mitzvot* such as Sabbath prohibitions, dietary laws, or candle lighting.

Religiousness has neither mass nor length. Unlike book knowledge, one cannot conclude that a testee knows none of it, half of it, or all of it. Quantification of religiousness rests on what Weber termed an *ideal-type* concept. The ideal type is defined as the phenomenon considered in its purest or most extreme form. The degree to which an observed belief or practice departs from the ideal defines the "amount" of religiousness. The Jewish ideal type tends to be interpreted as the traditionally normative belief or practice. As long as the scale is so labeled, no one need quarrel with it. It tells how orthodox the individual is.

A Reform Jew is not an irreligious Orthodox Jew but one who has rejected the legitimacy of halakhic authorities (such rejection de facto is not absent among members of Orthodox and Conservative congregations). A measure specific to Reform Jewishness might include dimensions such as commitment to the universalizing of Judaism, or willingness to tolerate a range of prescriptive norms, or the extent to which ethical judgment is legitimated with reference to prophetic principles. Some measure of religious experience or spirituality might not be out of place. Contemporary sociologists, perhaps squeamish about nonoccurring ideals, amend the ideal-type procedure to produce a self-anchoring scale. Such a scale establishes its own zero point on the basis of the distribution of responses actually obtained from some model population. Scales distinguish the relatively more religious from the relatively less religious. A given scale score could indicate varying degrees of religiousness in several populations with differing response distributions. The measure of religiousness becomes population specific.

The measure of religiousness in a given population should not be a function of the particular indicator items selected. If the responses meet the test of Guttman scalability (or unidimensionality), the selected items are thereby considered to sample properly the universe of possible items. Whichever the items chosen, Simon will always be classed as relatively more religious than Reuben—except when the difference between Simon and Reuben is less than the difference between scale types.

In practice, researchers pick items that will provide a reasonable distribution of scale types for the population being studied. Thus, the recent New York Jewish population study asked about fasting on the tenth of Teveth, a discriminator for a seriously religious part of the population. This item would not fulfill that function in any other American Jewish community study.

A ritual observance scale indicates the intersects between Jewish religiousness and other institutional commitments. Home rituals, lighting Sabbath candles, or holding a Seder say something about religion in the family and community. Saying kaddish says something about an attitude toward the continuity of the family and the religious community, among other things.

Some researchers look beyond the configured responses of a scale type and examine response to individual items. They must be cautioned that the meaning of a particular response is dependent on the configuration of responses. An individual who has a Seder and also has a kosher home and fasts on the tenth of Teveth probably holds a halakhically pure Seder, using the traditional Haggadah and leading into a most kosher Passover season. On the other hand, the person who has a Seder but does none of the other things in the scale may break a piece of matzah, not read any text or discuss any Passover topic, and may even serve French bread at the Seder table.

In the above example, the general social psychological concept of religiousness is tailored for Jewry by including items referring to Jewish practices. This describes religiousness as a form of motivation, energy invested in objects or activities deemed religious. Aside from ritual practices, one might base a measure on the willingness to risk oneself for Jewishness, the intensity of affirmation of Torah principles or the willingness to participate in building the Land of Israel. Another option, not yet examined, is to rest the measure on the distinctive Jewish attitude toward the clean and the unclean. The strength of the menstrual taboo, one indicator of such an attitude, could be an indicator of religious commitment.

The energy of faith itself, the drive, may be thought of in veridically Jewish terms. These include *haradah* (awe), *m'sirut* (devotion), and *hitlahavut* (enthusiasm). The possibilities for measuring Jewish religiousness based on Jewish types of commitment to Jewish values have hardly been tapped.

Of Time and Jewry

Social history, including that of Jewish life, does not unfold in linear time. Social time is measured by sociocultural activities and organizations. A shift between social forms marks a period in history. The definitions of the boundaries of Jewry and of the measure of Jewish religiousness may shift from one period to another. More often than not the period marker is a change in the dominant political system.

A period juncture may be a point at which a single community becomes two. The differentiation may follow a migration in response to economic interests or forced evacuation. Each of the successor communities proceeds on its own social clock. The Babylonian exile marks the beginning of the Babylonian Jewry as separate from the continuing Palestinian community. When, in the first century B.C., the latter community was establishing its academies, preparing ideas for the Mishnah, the Mesopotamian community, still free of Rome and intellectually asleep, awaited its time in the sun. Amoraim, exegetes of the Mishnah, and the Gaonim flowered in the environs of Baghdad. The Palestinian community was in decline.

The differentiation may be social structure, a community schism around ideological tendencies. The division between Jewish Christians and Pharisaic Jews in the second century was of this character. The Karaite-Rabbinite schism in the ninth and tenth centuries is another example.

Social time for each community is measured by the unfolding events of social change in the community. Damascene Jewry in the eighteenth century moved in slow historical time. The clock was turning rapidly for Prussian Jewry in that same century. Indeed, the periods or stages of development of the several Jewries of the world have not coincided.

Development, which need not imply progress, refers to change in social organization. Development is a change in a bounded and structured social entity. An *overall* periodization for a society assumes that it is a single social system. By any accepted sociological definition of society (a self-sufficient social system having relatively integrated political, economic, kin, and religious, among other, social subsystems), the Jews of the world have rarely met the criteria. The tribal prehistory, if considered a part of Jewish history, the periods of the commonwealths, and the current State of Israel meet the criteria of a bounded social system for Jews included in those societies. The Jewries under the united empires of Persia or Rome approach the status of societies though lacking political sovereignty.

Hungarian Jewish society, as an example, has had its own developmental sequence as a subordinate society. Beginning with a prehistory of trade and settlement around the Danube, Hungarian Jews enter a period of Magyar political hegemony around the tenth century. A short Eastern orientation during the Turkish occupation precedes the emergence of a relatively independent Jewish community strengthened by an influx of Western and Central European Yiddish-speaking Jews. In time, these immigrants carved out circles of domination among the indigenous Hungarians. By the late eighteenth century what had been a religiously homogeneous community evolved its urbanized *Neolog* (the modernizing counterpoint to Orthodoxy), religious reformationist tendencies which emerged under the modernizing patronage of the Hapsburgs. Eventually even a Marxist sub-community, manifest under Bela Kun's leadership of the Hungarian Soviets in the post-World War II years (or, perhaps, Bela Kun was more a Hungarian of Jewish descent than an identifying Jew) stood aside from the main body of the community. The Holocaust ended one period and opened a new one. The Jewish community of Hungary following World War I became part of a weak net of communities within the communist block of nations and minimized its ties with Western and Israeli Jewries. Jewish societies or communities contemporary with each other in a single empire or a national state may coalesce into a transcultural entity and share periodization. Thus, the Jews of Fez and of Andalusia were bound together under the Almohad caliphate.

Periods in the developmental history of Jewries subordinate to larger societies may, but need not, coincide with periods of the host societies. To understand contemporary Jewry, we refer to, without fully adopting, the social and cultural time of the peoples of which Jews are a part. The sociologist of Diaspora Jewry is also the sociologist of the rest of the world.

Yet, the environing society's periods may not be assigned mechanically to Jewish society. Antebellum is not a category in American Jewish history nor is postrevolutionary a category in the history of French Jewry. In Europe, however, postrevolutionary, although not a category of Jewish history, is relevant to periodization in Jewish history. Change in the European political climate facilitated modernizing movements within Jewry. In this way, the failure of the Continental revolutions of 1848 are significant for the development of American Jewry. They precipitated German-Jewish immigration to North America, marking a shift from Sephardic to Ashkenazic hegemony and to a more entrepreneurial commercial and industrial economy of American Jewry.

The various institutions of a society may develop and retrench at different rates and the periodization of institutional history will reflect this. Religion, literature, and law may each have their own developmental periods. The special evolution of these subsystems is due to the different exigencies, internal and external, to which each is responding. Take an example of Jewish literary history. The rabbinic hegemony over formal Jewish culture begins in the second century B.C. and is only now subsiding. The Tannaitic, Amoraic, and a later period of reinterpretation and collating involving Saadia Gaon, through the Rambam to Joseph Karo, is a literary sequence. The penetration of these literary themes into the general society is another matter. On the other hand, the economic life of Jewry followed another trajectory. The shift from agriculture to trade as a dominant motif is associated with the Roman period. Diaspora Jewry retained international trading as a significant community activity until industrial capitalism provided a meaningful alternative.

Jewish society moves in jagged time—sometimes lurching forward and sometimes falling backward in developmental level. The Jewish navigator maintains a fix on a continuing and unique Jewish past, the azimuth and altitude of which shift with the observer's own change of position.

Of the Blind and the Jewish Elephant

Sociological methodology complements the methodologies of psychology, anthropology, or political science, among others, in the scientific study of personality, society, and culture. Respectively, we may think of a psychology of Jews, an anthropology of Jews, and so forth. Each perspective reveals an aspect of Jewry. Humanistic study strives to identify Jewry's unique cultural expression. The specialization of sociology for Jewish society is inspired by the humanist's findings. Jewish social policy requires knowledge drawn from scientific and humanistic perspectives.

The decline of dialogue between the humanistic scholars of Judaism and the social scientific scholars of Jewry is puzzling. It is not puzzling as an empirical problem; factors such as increasing volume and density, to use Durkheim's word, of the academy have promoted specialization. The current dominance of science and technology, with government support, has pushed the scientific study of society along its own trajectory at a faster pace than that of the humanistic. What is puzzling is that the practitioners of the arts and sciences, including those concerned with Jewry, tolerate the split. Is the content of culture independent of the social forms in which it is structured? Is the inner integrity of a culture understandable in isolation from its external relations with other cultural systems? Does the study of the literary product of a cultural elite exhaust our knowledge of culture? What is the cultural status of the operative norms of everyman's society?

Nobody can know everything, but what we have to know depends on our question. A knowledge of Rabbinics is necessary to respond intelligently to a question about changing manifest functions of Jewish religious leadership. A knowledge of forces shaping the occupational structure of Jews is necessary for the changing social origins of Jewish leaders.

Sometimes the scholar uses the general sociological concepts to array the Jewish instance against the experience of the world. At other times, the scholar uses concepts specialized for the study of Jewry. Disciplines and methodologies are not additive. They may be mutually enlightening. Perhaps, if many blind students touch many parts of the Jewish elephant, someone may achieve the overview that discovers the pachyderm. Yes, it is a good idea to promote intellectual ties between the sociology of Jewry and the humanistic study of Judaism, secular and religious.

Postscript

Readers of *Contemporary Jewry* will have recognized my intellectual agenda in writing this paper. The article stakes out my position that a sociology of Jewry must be more "positive" than "normative," that the discipline must maintain its position within the mainstream of social science without surrendering its uniquely specialized character, and that the study of contemporary Jewry should not be isolated from the study of four thousand years of Jewish social history.

Notes

This paper is a revised and expanded version of a paper originally presented at the special conference Judaic Studies: Universal or Particular Contributions to Understanding World Civilization, sponsored by the Center for Judaic Studies and Contemporary Jewish Life, University of Connecticut, Storrs, 1982.
1. Specification of a concept may be distinguished from its "materialization." The latter refers to an hypostasis or intentional reification of an abstract idea, allowing it to represent the palpable world. The abstract notion of stratification is reified in revolutionary ideology to point to real, and unjust, inequalities among classes of people. "Materialization" is necessary for applying scientific findings in formulating social policy. Some sociologists of Jewry recommend Jewish social policy. They are applied social researchers in both senses. This essay confines itself to the first type of application, the specification of general sociological concepts for the study of Jewry.

2. Ascription is the rule by which the status is allocated by the group, a quality assigned by the society irrespective of the activities of the individual. Is this a vote for considering Jewishness a state of being, at least a socially ascribed state of being? No, because once the status is assigned, certain performances are expected—the male to be head of household in a patriarchal society; the son to honor his parents, supporting them when they become infirm; and the pope to shepherd his flock. We know that these performances are expected and judged because the group retains the right to sanction the status occupant, including the right to allocate the status to another person. Sons have been disowned and counter-popes established. Jews may be placed under a *herem*, excommunicated.

7

Theoretical Issues in the Sociology of Contemporary Jewries: Comments on "What Is Conceptually Special about a Sociology of Jewry"

Calvin Goldscheider

Theoretical and methodological issues associated with the sociological study of Jewry have rarely been articulated and almost never addressed systematically. To be sure, there are selected theories about Jews and their communities and an increasing number of research studies using diverse methodological strategies to investigate selected sociological aspects of Jews in various places and times. All too often the theories available and the empirical research carried out are not integrated or woven together methodologically. We lack conceptual frameworks, theoretical maps, to fit the various pieces together, to locate the particular within the general, or to know what is missing from our sociological analyses of Jewry. Hence, the sociological study of Jews in modern society has been the accident of person and subject: a topic is interesting, a sociologist is interested, so a particular research issue is pursued. There is little logic to the choice, no organized or sustained research focus, little coordination and cumulation of effort. As an intellectual, scholarly, and academic enterprise, the sociological study of Jewry has been the stepchild both of Jewish studies and the social sciences (see Goldscheider and Zuckerman 1984b).

In the past decade or so there has been an avalanche of studies on Jews in various communities, within different societies, that is unprecedented in history (see the reviews in Sklare 1982; Goldscheider and Zuckerman 1984a; Heilman 1982; Cohen et al. 1984). Although attempts to deal with research issues—for example, in selected areas of American community studies—have been made, there has been no comparable attempt to clarify the theoretical and conceptual issues that should guide empirical research. Hence, the goals set out by Samuel Klausner focusing on what is conceptually special about a sociology of Jewry are particularly important. His objective is to deal with a series of theoretical and methodological issues in the sociology of Jewry. Unfortunately, his orientation is not linked to specific research nor does he provide clear guidelines for investigating historical or comparative analytic themes in the study of contemporary Jews and their communities.

Rather than presenting a systematic critique and evaluation of Klausner's argument, I want to focus on these analytic themes and deal with some of the issues he raises in a different sociological mode. In the process an alternative view of the sociological theory tied to comparative research on contemporary Jewry will emerge. Dialogue on these issues, I believe, will result in a more systematic articulation of commonalities and differences among perspectives and will sharpen the understanding of these and other theoretical and methodological orientations. If the dialogue results in systematically incorporating theoretical and methodological issues in our research, the sociological study of Jewry will be enriched.

Sociology, in particular, and the social sciences, more generally, provide a perspective that is fundamental not only for the study of Jewry but for understanding human society in all of its manifestations, and can be applied to all societies at all points in time. Scholars have applied them to the study of the biblical period; others have used social scientific theories to map out issues of the Mishnah and the Talmud and to study Jews, their communities and cultures, at distant times and places. I and my social science colleagues use sociological and social scientific perspectives to study contemporary Jews and their communities. Although I agree with the conclusion of Samuel Klausner's paper that the study of contemporary Jewry "should not be isolated from the study of four thousand years of Jewish social history," I doubt whether that represents either a research or theoretical agenda. It is hardly justifiable, conceptually or methodologically, for students of contemporary Jewry to integrate their analyses into what would undoubtedly be a superficial framework of world Jewish history. It is not at all clear how sociological analyses of contemporary Jewry would be enriched by reference to biblical or talmudic history any more than sociological analyses of modern French society would be enhanced by the integration of thousands of years of the history of Western civilization. Therefore, I shall confine this essay to theoretical and methodological issues focused on Jews in modern societies (and to the processes associated with the transition to modern societies) because I do not think it necessary to cover the broad spectrum of Jews everywhere, at all points in time. Indeed, to phrase the question "of time and Jewry" in terms of the periodization of history, as does Klausner, is to focus on the problems of history and the variety of implications (ideological and historical) such periodization implies (see Kochan 1985). But the sociological question is not when does the modern period begin but, rather, how do the processes of modernization and transformation unfold. And, in turn, we analyze the determinants and consequences of these processes for the lives of people, for the institutions of society and the structure of social relations, and for the generational transmission of Jewish values and culture.

What, then, are the major analytic themes in the social scientific study of the Jews? The master theme of contemporary social science is the anaysis of the transformation of societies and the variety of groups within them as a result of modernization. Industrialization, urbanization, mobilization, secularization, and other changes are key elements. New structures and values, new institutions, ways of behaving and thinking, new jobs, residences, political movements, cultures, and ideologies, as well as new sources of conflict, competition, and inequalities have emerged in the modern era. Our master question then becomes: What has been the impact of these transformations on the Jews? How has the modernization of the societies in which Jews lived affected them? How have Jews, their leaders and elites, and their organizations and institutions responded to the sweep of modernization? With the dissolution of the older bases of cohesion, what new types of communal bonds, associational ties, and cultural forms link Jews to one another? What are the bases of solidarity, in the Durkheimian sense, among Jews and their communities as they were transformed by modernization?

These questions focus our attention on broad changes over time and their effects on Jews and their communities. History has a central place in sociological analyses of Jews; not the four-thousand-year history of Jews everywhere, but historical processes associated with the transformation of Jews in modern societies. We are concerned about those particular processes associated with modernization, not about all historical change. So our focus is not on an abstract and oversimplified notion of historical events and sequences but in the processes associated with the modernization of societies, communities, families, and individuals.

Our questions, therefore, involve, first and foremost, a focus on historical change of a particular sociological kind. They also require a second, related type of comparison in addition to changes over time: variation across communities within and between countries. The objective of cross-community and historical comparisons is not to isolate the exotic and unique; rather, it is to frame analytic questions (why changes occur in community X and not in community Y) and to provide a comparative basis for testing theories and hypotheses with empirical evidence.

We can focus solely on the Jews and their communities, analyzing their patterns over time and in various communities. We can learn much from such "internal" group comparisons, but these alone are insufficient to address systematic analytic themes in the social sciences. We need to make a third, related type of comparison through the systematic inclusion of non-Jews in our analysis of the Jews. Ideally, we would want to compare systematically Jews and the many groups of non-Jews over time and in various societies. Such comparisons provide the basis for evaluating the structural and cultural sources of Jewish distinctiveness and assessing whether differences between Jews and non-Jews are temporary and transitory or whether they are embedded in social structure.

It is clearly not appropriate analytically to compare Jews with non-Jews without taking into account and disentangling differential structural *and* cultural patterns. Thus, for example, comparing Jews in Germany in the nineteenth century with all Germans without taking into account the specific jobs, urban location, and education of the Jews would be misleading. Such a crude comparison would reveal differences between Jews and non-Jews, reflecting in large part social-class and rural-urban residential differences but not necessarily specific factors associated with Jewishness or Judaism, the place of Jews in German society, or their "culture." On the one hand, to know that differrences between Jews and non-Jews in nineteenth-century Germany are primarily the consequence of socioeconomic and demographic differences shapes a series of specific analytic questions regarding the determinants and consequences of the particular socioeconomic and demographic characteristics of German Jewry. On the other hand, in neutralizing the socioeconomic and demographic effects, we are able to focus on other powerful structural and cultural factors. But simply to attribute crude differences between Jews and non-Jews to "culture" and "values" particular to Jews without taking into account the social structural, demographic, and economic bases of our comparisons results in a series of distortions in our understanding of social change among Jews in Europe and the United States over the past century (for examples see the discussion in Goldscheider and Zuckerman 1984a; Steinberg 1981; Goldscheider 1984). Thus, multiple comparisons—historical, cross-community, and with non-Jews—are the bases for the systematic sociological analyses of Jews and their communities. Without comparisons, we are left with description, not analysis, and no basis for testing theories and hypothesis.

The structural and cultural questions we ask of societies in general and of subgroups within society are those that we ask of Jews and their communities. But why focus on the Jews? Are there analytic considerations, beyond issues of self-interest and ethnocentrism that justify our investigation of the Jews? If not, general sociologists will learn little from our sociology of the Jews and we will address only one another. I submit that it is more fruitful analytically to address questions about the processes of transformation to the Jewish group than to total societies because comparative analysis is facilitated by the central role Jews have played in the areas of earlier and later modernization within Europe and in the new nations of the United States and Israel. The comparative study of Jews thus provides a handle for understanding general processes of Western development. The location of Jews in various societies makes it efficient to examine comparatively changes across societies. Focusing on society as a whole involves significant heterogeneity and internal variation, often masking crucial patterns; cross-societal comparisons only compound these analytic difficulties. And although the Jews occupy a unique position in Western societies, insights derived from a sociological analysis of the Jews are generalizable to others when the focus is on analytic issues within comparative and historical perspectives (see Goldscheider and Zuckerman 1984a).

Issues of modernization apply to Jews and their communities as they apply to total societies and other ethnic and minority groups. The examination of the transformation of the Jews yields insight as well into critical theories associated with the social, political, economic, and cultural integration of minority, ethnic, and religious groups in the processes associated with modernization, including social differentiation, communal cohesion, intergroup relations, and the structural and cultural dimensions of assimilation. Important aspects of the core theories of ethnicity in pluralistic societies can be systematically tested within the framework of the sociology of the Jews (see, for example, Goldscheider 1986). There are, in addition, particular Jewish issues of modernization that are of importance in exploring modern Jewish society. These include the specifics of Judaism, anti-Semitism, and the internal structure and organization of the Jewish community.

In the modernization of the Jews, their religion was transformed. The normative and communal centrality of Judaism declined. As the older order changed, so did the institutions legitimating that order. As religion changed, it was redefined and new forms of communal identification emerged. How these changes evolve, what becomes the bases of the new forms of legitimacy and consensus, and how cultural and value consensus emerge are key issues. The responses of religious movements and ideologies to the challenges of modern secular society and in relation to other social-religious movements require clarification. The transformation from religious centrality to communal ethnic diversity poses the fundamental concern for Jewish continuity and discontinuity at the community and individual levels. Clearly, religiosity (or religiousness) is not only or primarily an issue of "personal commitment to specifically religious institutions" or ideologies, as Klausner suggests. It is social and communal. These broader contexts are often lost when the sociologies of Judaisms are discussed solely in the context of their formal ideologies and organizational patterns and not in terms of the social definitions of membership and identification, family and generation patterns. Klausner's example of saying kaddish as reflecting "an attitude toward the continuity of the family and the religious community" places too much emphasis on the attitudinal and personal components of religiosity and minimizes the enormous social, institutional, and network patterns associated with kaddish saying and other seemingly individual rituals. His other illustrations of measuring Jewish religiosity in terms of the "energy and faith" of Judaism and other religious acts, attitudes, and beliefs appear to me to miss the critical dimensions of the sociology of religiosity in modern societies.

Sociologists of Jewry, Klausner argues, "rarely ask a Jewish question, that is, one framed by ideas formed in Jewish experience." Yet, his illustrations of Judaic concepts of purity and covenant leading to distinctly Judaic ways of thinking about belongingness, identity, and obligation are not likely to be a framework for sociological research of today's or yesterday's Jews. It might be an appropriate question for a theology or an intellectual history of contemporary Jews, but Klausner provides no basis for assuming that these concepts are helpful, theoretically, methodologically, or empirically, in the *sociological* study of Jews. Indeed, I would argue that the "Jewish *verstehende*" does not require, as Klausner suggests, Jewish principles of order guiding the observed social relations of Jews but a sociological *verstehende* grounded in the rich sociological tradition of Weber, Marx, and Durkheim, among others.

A second particular feature in the analysis of modern Jewish society relates specifically to anti-Semitism and ethnic-religious discrimination in general. How important are attitudes, policies, and ideologies of governments and of non-Jews in understanding the transformation of the Jews? How does political anti-Semitism relate to various ideologies and governments? How does anti-Semitism in its political and attitudinal forms relate to conflict, competition, and inequality within societies? How is anti-Semitism affected by the presence of other minorities in the society? How are political and attitudinal dimensions of anti-Semitism related to each other and to the attitudes and values of non-Jews and Jews? How do these dimensions relate to the size and structure of the Jewish community? These questions are particular to Jews, in ways that are perhaps different for Jews than for religious, ethnic, and racial minorities in general. These features of Jewish social life are conspicuously underdeveloped in Klausner's presentation. Can there be a comprehensive sociology of the Jews without taking into consideration the political, social, and attitudinal context of non-Jewish "others"?

The changing internal structure of the Jewish community, its variation across societies, and the relationship of Jews to institutions and organizations that are the formal network of the community are the final arena of specific analytic concern. Clearly the organization of the Jewish community is transformed in the process of modernization. How and why the formal structure changes and what the role of ideological factors is in shaping those changes are major questions. How these institutional changes are linked to, determine, and are the consequence of changes in the social structure of the Jewish community are critical issues. How does the organizational structure of the Jewish community link to the formal organizational and institutional structure of the general community? In short, the sources of growth, expansion, and competition among organizations and the emergence of new institutions need to be analyzed in the broader contexts of organizational theory and other institutional developments occurring in society. As organizations and institutions change, so do elites; as the centrality of religion declines, so does the authority and power of the rabbis; as religion takes on new forms and new secular and religious organizations are shaped, new organizational elites emerge with new sources of power and new bases of resources. The linkages between religious and secular organizational developments within the Jewish community and the changing relationships between ethnic and religious dimensions of Jewish identity and identification are prime theoretical and empirical areas of inquiry.

These are complex issues that relate to Jews specifically and to changes in the place of Jews in modern society. In large part these issues revolve around the forces shaping why particular changes occur among Jews and how Jews respond similarly to and differently than non-Jews. But we ask questions not only about the determinants of changes among Jews but about the consequences of these changes for Jewish continuity. More particularly, we focus on the implications of the transformation of the Jewish community for the relative cohesion of the Jewish community. We analyze the relative cohesion of communities under different conditions; we should not infer the *implications* of change from the changing characteristics of the Jewish community. Thus, for example, the increasing secularization of Judaism has been documented in almost every study of the modernization of Jewish communities. Often, the inference has been made that patterns of secularization have negative consequences for the cohesion of the Jewish community; from the point of view of the community, therefore, secularization is one indicator of the decline of the Jewish community in modern society. That is the case only when we confuse Judaism with Jewishness and equate the religion of the Jews with the nature of the Jewish community. These dimensions were more interchangeable in the past, when religion was more central in the lives of Jews and connected in integral ways to social, economic, family, cultural, and political aspects of Jewish communities. In modern pluralistic societies, the two questions have to be untangled: (1) How are changes in religion linked to other processes of modernization? and (2) What are the implications of secularization patterns for the cohesion of the community?

If the cohesion of the Jewish community is defined by the religiosity of the Jewish community, then a decline in religiosity implies a decrease in Jewish cohesion, by definition. Rabbis and theologians often confuse the two. Social scientists cannot. If religion is but one component of Jewish cohesion, what are the other elements? Here is my sharpest disagreement with Klausner. He has framed the "uniqueness" of Jewry in terms of "Jewish cultural values." Specifically, he states, "Jewry is that social group in which members share an expectation of action in concert in support of what are considered to be Jewish values." And he adds, "The centrality of Torah . . . is the foundation for the centrality of peoplehood." By extension this would mean that the extent of uniqueness, i.e. the cohesion of Jewry, relates first and foremost to the relative importance of Jewish values and Torah in the shared expectations of those who are members of the social group. But there are a variety of arenas of social life where social interaction can provide the bases for defining Jewish cohesion. I would argue for this broader social structural view of Jewish cohesion. Hence, the greater the interaction among Jews with Jews rather than with others in a larger number of arenas of social life, the more cohesive is the community. This neither precludes or deemphasizes the study of Jewish values. It focuses our attention on value consensus among Jews as *one* factor among many in Jewish communal life; it directs our attention to the social, economic, and political conditions under which there is greater or lesser consensus about values; it treats values not primarily as determinants but as consequences of social structure. The relationships between values, Jewish and general, and other forms of Jewish cohesion become theoretical and empirical issues, not simply assertions.

Multiple comparisons among Jews and between Jews and others are necessary to move beyond description. Emphasis on behavior and on the characteristics of Jews and their communities needs to be separated from an analysis of values and attitudes, if only to see how behavior and values are related. The study of elites, norms, ideologies, and ideas is important but should not be viewed as substitutes for analyzing the behavior of the masses and the characteristics of their communities. The elite, by definition, is not a cross-section of the community. To study the elite, comparatively and historically, is a most engaging area of investigation but it is not the same as studying the Jewish community. Norms, values, and ideas are not synonymous with behavior. Values, ideologies, and culture need to be studied as phenomena to be explained no less than as sources of explanation. Indeed, there is a critical need to test the relative importance of structural and cultural explanations of social processes, no less among Jews than in general sociological analyses. Elite ideas are but one of many determinants of mass behavior; indeed, they are rarely the only determinants of the behavior of elites.

We need to ask theoretical questions to guide our empirical inquiries and identify new areas of comparative research among contemporary Jews and their communities. It is a grand intellectual challenge and a complex scholarly agenda to place the sociological study of the Jews in the broader context of the societies of which they are a part, to examine the unique and the general, to test theories and hypotheses, to investigate the general social, economic, cultural, and political patterns of the Jews and their communities, and to see connections among communities, comparing Jews and others systematically and over time. It is the agenda of the social services in general. It is doubly difficult when the focus is on Jews and their communities because of the need to investigate one group among many and to link their analysis with other groups, other Jews, and societal patterns in general. The permutations are extensive. Nevertheless, and perhaps because of it, it is an intellectual challenge of the highest order and worth pursuing.

The sociologies of the Jews are linked to the perspectives of other social sciences and to the humanities. On this we cannot but agree with Klausner. Yet that remains an incomplete assertion until we specify those links theoretically and methodologically. We need to put our own sociological house in order before we can approach those linkages and before we invite our humanist friends who study Judaism and Jewish history to visit and partake in the search for the grand integrative theories.

Notes

This paper draws on two recent research projects focusing on the comparative-historical analysis of contemporary Jews (Goldscheider and Zuckerman 1984a) and an analysis of the sociology of American Jews (Goldscheider 1986). My continuing research with Alan Zuckerman on the comparative study of Jews in modern societies informs the theoretical and methodological thrust of this paper. Frances K. Goldscheider read an earlier version and helped sharpen my presentation.

References

Cohen, S., et al., eds. 1984. *Perspectives in Jewish Population Research.* Boulder, Colo.: Westview Press.

Goldscheider, C. 1984. "Including Non-Jews in Jewish Community Surveys." In *Perspectives in Jewish Population Research*, ed. S. Cohen et al. Boulder, Colo.: Westview Press.

_____. 1986. *Jewish Continuity and Change: Emerging Patterns in America.* Bloomington: Indiana University Press.

Goldscheider, C., and A. Zuckerman. 1984a. *The Transformation of the Jews.* Chicago: University of Chicago Press.

_____. 1984b. "Contemporary Jewish Studies in the Social Sciences: Analytic Themes and Doctoral Studies." In *New Humanities and Academic Disciplines: The Case of Jewish Studies*, ed. J. Neusner. Madison: University of Wisconsin Press.

Heilman, S. 1982. "The Sociology of American Jewry: The Last Ten Years." *Annual Review of Sociology* 8:135-60.

Kochan, L. 1985. "The Methodology of Modern Jewish History." *Journal of Jewish Studies* 36:185-94.

Sklare, M., ed. 1982. *Understanding American Jewry.* New Brunswick, N.J.: Transaction Books.

Steinberg, S. 1981. *The Ethnic Myth: Race, Ethnicity, and Class in America.* New York: Atheneum.

8

Examples of What Klausner Calls "Good," "Mature" Sociology of Jewry

J. Alan Winter

Professor Klausner is correct, I believe, in reminding us that one sign that we "have achieved a mature sociology of Jewry when scholars not otherwise concerned with Jewry study Jews as part of a strategy for elaborating general sociological concerns . . . ." He is also correct in asserting that one type of "good study of Jewry" is that which evokes "Jewish ideas . . . [as] a basis for new general concepts which may be applied in the study of other[s] . . . ." However, given his concern with more general issues, Klausner does not himself cite specific examples of any such "mature" or "good" sociological study of Jewry. There are some, of course. I shall discuss two: Steinberg's (1965) study of the rise of the Reform movement, and Herberg's (1960) analysis of interreligious relationships in the Unitied States. The former is an example of a "mature" sociology of Jewry in that it is a study of Jews that elaborates a general sociological concern. The latter exemplifies a "good study" in that it evokes ideas based on Jewish thought as a basis for general concepts applicable to groupings other than Jews.

Steinberg's Study as "Mature" Sociology of Jewry

Steinberg (1965; 117) chose to study the origin and evolution of Reform Judaism because of "the difficulty of accommodating the Reform case to accepted sociological propositions concerning church and sect." The relevant propositions constitute what I have elsewhere (Winter 1977; 148-64) described as the "sect-to-church hypothesis." In summary terms, it holds that new religious movements begin as sectlike organizations in tension with the values and practices of the surrounding society, appealing to the lower class, but develop into churchlike organizations comfortable with the surrounding society, appealing to the middle-class. The sect-to-church hypothesis does, of course, fit the broad outlines of the history of many

Protestant denominations, especially those that arose in the nineteenth and twentieth centuries, as shown in Niebuhr's (1929) classic study. Moreover, it conforms to much of Christian self-understanding. That is, the hypothesis is consistent with the common Christian view that Christianity began as a sect despised by Jews and Romans alike, only to develop later into the dominant institution of Western society. In short, the sect-to-church hypothesis is supported by the broad outlines of a good bit of Christian history.

Nevertheless, Steinberg's attempts to apply the sect-to-church hypothesis to a study of Reform Judaism leads him, as Klausner suggests may happen when general sociological concepts are applied to Jewish experience, to an elaboration and clarification of the original concept. The result is a "mature" sociological study of Jewry, one of interest to scholars not otherwise concerned with Jewry.

Steinberg defines *church* and *sect* as polar types on a continuum extending from low to high tension with the surrounding society. In so doing, he follows Johnson's (1963) modification of Troeltsch's sect-church typology. However, Steinberg (p. 119) finds it necessary to elaborate on Johnson's definition by distinguishing between two types of religious organizations: the institution and the rump group (schismatic group). The former is simply defined as "a religious organization that possesses property"; the latter, as a "group that severs its connections with the institution and thereby forsakes its rights to the property of the institution." The rump group may, of course, later acquire its own property and become, ipso facto, an institution. Steinberg then cross-classifies the institution and the rump group with Johnson's criterion of church and sect. He does so on the assumption that both the institution and the rump group may, as his study of the Reform movement suggests, come into either more or less tension with the surrounding environment over time. That is, Steinberg stresses that institutions do not always act as churches, nor all rump groups, as sects. For example, a rump group may upon its inception seek less tension with its surrounding society than has the group from which its splits, thereby moving itself in a churchlike direction. Such a rump group is called a "church movement" by Steinberg. The Reform movement began, according to Steinberg's analysis, as just such a church movement, that is, as a religious movement seeking to lessen the tension between it and the surrounding society. As Steinberg notes, "The Reform Movement is an anomaly among religious movements in that it sought to modify institutional norms and values that were discrepant with those of the larger society" (p. 120).

Importantly, Steinberg's attempt to deal with the anomaly may lead to an elaboration of the original sect-church concept of potential benefit in studies of non-Jewish groups. For example, it provides concepts that may be used to analyze the actions of an established institutionalized religion, such as the Roman Catholic Church, which may, at times, come into greater tension with its surrounding society, thereby moving in a sectlike direction. The church under John Paul II, for example, may be said to be moving in that direction regarding its position in the Western, industrialized societies as the pope increasingly criticizes modern values of family life that result in increased divorce, abortion, and contraception. Moreover, the distinction that Steinberg makes between institutions that retain property and rump groups, which do not, should prove more useful than the more restricted concepts of the original sect-church hypothesis in the study of such new religious organizations as the Anglican church, which was sprung fully grown from the head of King Henry VIII. Furthermore, the development of divisions within Islam, following the death of Mohammed, which do not conform to the sect-church hypothesis, may similarly be amenable to analysis in terms developed by Steinberg's "mature" sociological study of Jewry.

Herberg's Study as "Good" Sociology of Jewry

Herberg's now-classic study of the relationships of Protestants, Catholics, and Jews, whose overall value I have discussed elsewhere (Winter 1977; 197ff.), is a fine example of what Klausner calls "a good study of Jewry" in that it evokes Jewish ideas as a basis for new, general concepts of use in the study of non-Jews. The Jewish ideas evoked by Herberg, more implicitly perhaps than otherwise, are those pertaining to the difference between practice of the Jewish religion and membership in the Jewish community. That is, as Klausner suggests, commitment to a life according to Halakhah or to some other form of Jewish religiousness must be distinguished from other forms of Jewishness, such as ethnicity or nationalism. Thus, the distinction between Judaism as a religion and Jewishness as an ethnic phenomenon has become commonplace in studies of Jewry, albeit, as Klausner notes, the structurally separation of Judaism from other Jewish institutions is of rather recent origin. In any case, such a distinction is rare in studies of non-Jews.

One would be hard-pressed to identify a term that distinguishes between religious and nonreligious ways of being or acting Christian. In common parlance and in sociological studies, to be Christian is to be religious in some degree. That is, in the terms Klausner borrows from Rudolf Otto, the determination of whether one is a Christian or not involves determination of one's relationship to the *mysterium tremendum*, or in more general sociological terms, to what Durkheim termed the "sacred," viz., that which is set apart and forbidden. The term *Christian* refers to some form of religiousness. There are no "secular Christians" and no secular way to be Christian according to common parlance and standard, non-Herbergian, sociological terminology.

Herberg, however, provides a way to distinguish between Christian religious and nonreligious involvement. I believe he was able to make the distinction because of his familiarity with modern Jewish thought and practice. In any case, Herberg distinguishes between involvement in the Christian religion and involvement in a Christian, Protestant or Catholic, religious community. As he makes quite clear (1960;39), involvement in a religious community, whether Protestant, Catholic, or for that matter, Jewish, "does not in itself necessarily imply actual affiliation with a particular church, participation in religious activities, or even the affirmation of any definite creed or belief . . . ." To the contrary, involvement in a religious community is simply "a way of sociability or 'belonging'" (p. 260) that implies "identification and social location" (p. 39). More specifically, membership in a religious community is defined by involvement in primary relationships, e.g. by friendship, and dating and mating patterns, not by religious belief or practice. Thus, it is quite possible to be a member of the Catholic community but not the Catholic church, just as it is possible to be Jewish but reject the beliefs and practices of Judaism. There are, in Herberg's scheme, both secular Christians and as well secular Jews.

The sociological value of Herberg's distinction and analysis is, of course, primarily demonstrated by its heuristic value in generating further study and in providing a conceptual framework for analyzing a myriad of studies. Its value in this regard has already been discussed by others (e.g. Greeley 1972) and me (Winter 1977; 197ff.). The distinction may also be useful in providing a basis for a sociological analysis of practical (legal) issues in the United States, as I have shown (Winter 1977; 235-63). For example, Herberg's distinction between the religious community and the religious congregation (church or synagogue) may be useful in understanding recent controversy concerning the appropriateness of certain Christmas displays on public property.

The Supreme Court (1984) ruled in *Lynch v. Donnelly* that a display that includes such things as a Santa Claus house, reindeer, candy-striped poles, carolers, a clown, an elephant, a teddy bear, colored lights, and a "Seasons Greetings" banner does not constitute a religious display despite the inclusion of a creche. Most people, including the majority of the Court, would, I think, agree that the display was in some sense "Christian." In pre-Herbergian terms and in common parlance the display would, ipso facto, be religious. In such terms to be "Christian" is to be religious. However, in Herberg's terms such is not necessarily the case. Something may be Christian by virtue of its relationship to the Christian community, that is, by virtue of a connection to primary relationships among Christians, without necessarily being religious—just as bagels and lox, by virtue of their relationship to the Jewish family, is "Jewish" without being "Judaic." Thus, the Supreme Court and those who agree with it are in effect saying that many aspects of Christmas celebration, whatever their origins, are now practiced as adjuncts to family life and are no longer any more religious than, say, the practice of trick-or-treating at Halloween, sending flowers on St. Valentine's Day, or for that matter honoring thy mother and thy father on Mother's and Father's Day, respectively. In any case, whatever the specific merits, or lack thereof, of the Supreme Court ruling on the constitutionality of Christmas displays on public property, Herberg's study of Protestants, Catholics and Jews in the United States remains a bit of "good" sociology of Jewry, as Klausner defines the term, because it invokes ideas rooted in Jewish experience as a basis for general concepts applicable to the study of non-Jews as well.

It may well be hoped that Klausner's timely reminder will spur others to follow Steinberg and Herberg in the conduct of good and mature sociological studies of Jewry. We all, Jew and gentile, sociologist and layperson, will be the better for it.

References

Greeley, Andrew M. 1972. *The Denominational Society*. Glenview, Ill.: Scott, Foresman.

Herberg, Will. 1960. *Protestant—Catholic—Jew*. Garden City, N.Y.: Doubleday.

Johnson, Benton. 1963. "On Church and Sect." *American Sociological Review* 28: 539-49.

Niebuhr, H. Richard. 1929. *The Social Sources of Denominationalism*. New York: Holt, Reinhart & Winston.

Steinberg, Stephen. 1965. "Reform Judaism: Origin and Evolution of a Church Movement." *Journal for the Scientific Study of Religion* 5:117-29.

Supreme Court of the United States. 1984. *Lynch, Mayor of Pawtucket et al. v. Donnelley et al.* 82-1256 (slip opinion).

Winter, J. Alan. 1977. *Continuities in the Sociology of Religion*. New York: Harper & Row.

9

The Conceptually Separate: The Need for a Dynamic Relationship between Comparative Science and Particularist Scholarship—A Response to Klausner

Walter P. Zenner

The appearance of an article dealing with the basic issue of how social science is best applied to Jewish and/or Judaic materials is welcome. For a sociocultural anthropologist it is gratifying to see that the kind of approach that Klausner advocates is exemplified by my discipline. Anthropologists have made the diversity of human ways their special concern. Because of this they have been more sensitive to the worldviews of their subjects than to *a priori* theories, often based upon the investigator's common sense but presumed to have universal validity. This does not mean that anthropologists have been successful in all instances. The search for cross-cultural generalizations calls for concepts and categories that are applicable outside any specific culture, even if this violates the intracultural usage of such a concept. In this brief communication I will respond to Klausner's concerns from the viewpoint of an anthropologist interested both in the problem of cross-cultural comparison, using Jewish materials, and one who has studied specific Jewish cultures.

Klausner's discussion of social science as an outgrowth of a specific cultural tradition calls our attention to a truism, which is very easy to forget. It is almost impossible to transcend this tradition fully, for if we did we would not be social scientists.

That the categories we use are ways of seeing is a point that cannot be stressed too often. Although Western Christian and rationalist biases inhere in these concepts, social scientists always bring their prototypes of their particular subjects to their conceptualiztions. A course in race and ethnic relations will be taught in one way if the key problem is that of anti-Semitism, another if it is Black-White relations in the United States and

South Africa, and differently still if "tribalism" in Africa and communalism in South Asia are at its heart. The kinds of explanation of interethnic hostility based on irrationality, theology, and competition make sense for the interpretation of anti-Semitism, and notions of exploitation and racial inferiority are central to explanations of Black-White relations. Even in the more limited area of "middleman minorities," one finds that the focus changes when the prototype is that of Japanese-Americans from what it was when it was on European Jews (Bonacich 1973 and 1980; Porter 1981; Zenner 1978 and 1980). European Jews and Japanese Americans differ in a number of formal characteristics. For instance, truck farming was a major occupation for pre-World War II Japanese Americans, but such occupations were not as important among the Jews. Jews had been in several of the European countries for many centuries; the Japanese Americans were relatively recent immigrants.

The historical dimension in middleman minorities is quite significant when comparing Jews with others in that category. Most groups labeled "middleman minorities," including the Overseas Chinese, the South Asians, and the Armenians, were supported in the past by a peasant hinterland; the Jewish dispersion sustained itself without relying on sources of peasant migrants (Zenner 1983). Thus, the dynamics of sojourning has a different meaning when applied to Jews than to others. Here the point that Klausner makes about how different is the time perspective of Jewish history from that of others becomes relevant.

Klausner suggests that the application of non-Jewish models to the Jews is misleading, but the reverse can also be true. A view of genocides modeled on the Holocaust may be misleading in interpreting the Armenian "Holocaust" in Anatolia during World War I. Relations between Christians and Muslims in the Arab countries, including Lebanon, are quite different from relations between Jews and Gentiles in Eastern and Central Europe before World War II. Analogies between these situations draw on the basis of the Jewish experience in Europe have been misleading. Although each of these situational analyses might be amplified by examination of the constructions of meanings in each circumstance, much of the work done on each would reveal important differences even if we concentrate on structural and economic factors alone.

The point that Klausner makes quite cogently is that we must utilize "native" or "actor's" models rather than those that the investigators carry with them from their own societies or from what has been taken into social science, often on the basis of a particular Western pattern. In the field of religion, both in comparative studies and in sociological research, the need to adapt to "native" categories while maintaining a cross-cultural perspective is of particular difficulty. The terms *religion, faith,* and *belief* are themselves intimately bound up with Protestant and Catholic worldviews. They are difficult to apply to other cultures, especially those outside the sphere of Abrahamic religions (Needham 1972; Smith 1964).

Other terms that anthropologists have taken from non-Western cultures and used for comparative purposes may also be misleading. For instance, Jewish food prohibitions, such as on the pig, differ from the avoidance of the pig, including mention of the name, by Scottish fishermen. Fraser (1919) associated the two, using the Polynesian concept of taboo. Steiner (1956:98-101) has, however, demonstrated that while Jews may have died for the sanctification of the Name to avoid eating pork, they—unlike the Scots—did not associate the use of the word for swine with any kind of magic. Thus the word *taboo* obscures the differences between the two avoidances.

Institutionally, Judaism and Islam differ from Christianity, and all three traditions contain important regional and sectarian variants. Although both social scientists and journalists use the term *clergy* to talk about Catholic priests, rabbis, protestant ministers, and the Islamic *ulema*, these specialists are not fully equivalent, either in terms of their statuses or roles. The sacramental functions of the Catholic priest are not found in the roles carried out by any of the other "clergy." Similarly, the term *church*, as both the all-embracing body of adherents and as a building found on the local level, is used differently from the term *bet knesset*. There are important variations within Judaism, so that the American synagogue center, which is based on a membership group and which provides a wide variety of sacred and secular services, is unique to North America. With regard to all these terms, social scientists benefit from a thorough semantical analysis.

In the area of values, attitudes, and norms, one may sense that Jews may share a similar stance with other groups, but it is difficult to put one's finger on it, whether it is a syndrome dealing with an overly protective and intrusive mother's relations with her children or an ethnic historiography marked by an emphasis on suffering. In dealing with the latter, I started with Baron's characterization of traditional Jewish attitudes toward the past as the "lachrymose conception of Jewish history" (1958:232-34). I sensed that other ethnic groups, such as the Irish, the Armenians, the Blacks, and American Indians had similar views toward their pasts. In translating one's intuition into proof, however, one realizes how one is often ignorant of the literatures of the other groups. This is particularly true when one must rely on translations. Thus, although the theme of lachrymosity transcends the Jews, more work must be done on how it has been used (Zenner 1977).

The theme of suffering that does appear in so many histories may be due to its appeal in story telling. There may be an appeal to the pathetic that makes those who suffer more attractive than those who do not. Suffering may add tension. For instance, in Japanese stories, dramas, and histories those who failed rather than those who won were often seen as the heroes, even though Japanese history has been less marked by foreign conquest than that of most other nations (Morris 1975). In Japanese history these noble losers represent generally themselves and did not symbolize the nation or an ideological cause until recent times. Comparison may mislead, but it can also help to deepen our understanding of a particular cultural theme.

Klausner proceeds from discussing such questions of research strategy to a consideration of the tactics of inquiry. He discusses these primarily with a view toward the construction of questionnaires. This is the technique favored by most positivistic sociologists, but it is not the only methodology available. In fact, from the viewpoint of cultural anthropology the questionnaire is seen as a technique that one uses to confirm results obtained through other methods using a large sample, rather than viewing it as the penultimate goal of inquiry. The preceding research is considered more significant than the questionnaire. Detailed description of settings and events, as well as the analysis of the structure and contents of texts and other discourses are much more suited to getting at the actors' views *in situ* than are questionnaires. These techniques are sensitive to nuances that we miss when we construct the questions ourselves. We can find texts that provide us with such views or even generate them, such as eliciting life histories.

The methods associated with observation can also be extended through ingenuity. Direct observations can be recorded by computers and by videocameras. Individuals may be asked to record activities and reactions at times selected by the researcher and they can be signaled to record by a beeper. Detailed semantical analyses can reveal verbal associations of different concepts, so that the connotations of significant terms are elicited. Just as Klausner advocates the release of the sociological study of Jewry from a Western-Christian or secular conceptual framework, so the sociology of Jewry must take off a methodological straitjacket.

Social scientists who utilize such a plethora of methods must, of course, resort to census results and to questionnaires. When they do, however, they will come to them with different perspectives. The questions that they ask would reflect a new perception of the actors' reality and pay more attention to activities and language than to opinions and attitudes. Through opening the study of Jewry to greater sensitivity to the Judaic view of the world, we can build a broader sociology of the Jews and Judaism, a sociology that will be conceptually distinct and yet provide a basis for probing the diverse shapes that human behavior can take.

References

Baron, Salo W. 1958. *A Social and Religious History of the Jews.* Vol. 6, *Laws, Homilies and the Bible.* New York: Columbia University Press.

Bonacich, Edna. 1973. "A Theory of Middleman Minorities." *American Sociological Review* 38:583-94.

————. 1980. "Middleman Minorities and Advanced Capitalism." *Ethnic Groups* 2:211-19.

Fraser, James. 1919. *Folklore of the Old Testament.* London: Macmillan.

Morris, Ivan. 1975. *The Nobility of Failure.* New York: Holt, Rinehart & Winston.

Needham, Rodney. 1972. *Belief, Language and Experience.* Chicago: University of Chicago Press.

Porter, Jack Nusan. 1981. "The Urban Middleman." *Comparative Social Research* 4:199-215.

Smith, Wilfred C. 1964. *The Meaning and End of Religion.* New York: New American Library.

Steiner, Franz. 1956. *Taboo.* Harmondsworth, U.K.: Penguin Books.

Zenner, Walter P. 1977. "Lachrymosity: A Cultural Reinforcement of Minority Status." *Ethnicity* 4:156-66.

————. 1978. Middleman Minority Theory and the Jews: A Historical Assessment. YIVO Working Papers in Yiddish and East European Jewish Studies No. 31.

————. 1980. "Middleman Minority Theories: A Critical Review." In *Sourcebook on the New Immigration,* ed. R.S. Bryce-Laporte, D. Mortimer, and S.R. Couch, pp. 411-25. New Brunswick, N.J.: Transaction.

————. 1983. "The Jewish Diaspora and the Middleman Adaptation." In *Diaspora: Exile and the Jewish Condition,* ed. E. Levine, pp. 141-56. New York: Jason Aronson.

REVIEW ESSAYS

This section inaugurates a new feature in Contemporary Jewry, *the publication of essays on books that might be regarded as most central to the social scientific study of Jewry. Where possible we have asked reviewers to write an essay on two books that appear to have a common theme. Following, then, are the contributions of our three reviewers, Steven Bayme, Harold S. Himmelfarb, and Carol Poll, who have reviewed five recent important books for our readers. Comments are invited on these review essays, and they may be published in future issues of* Contemporary Jewry. *In addition, suggestions as to books to be reviewed and persons to write the reviews are welcomed by the Editorial Office.*

10

Sociology of Talmud Study

The World of the Yeshiva: An Intimate Portrait of Orthodox Jewry,
by William B. Helmreich.
New York: Free Press, 1982. 412 pp. $19.95.

The People of the Book: Drama, Fellowship, and Religion,
by Samuel C. Heilman.
Chicago: University of Chicago Press, 1983. 337 pp. $22.50.

Reviewed by *Harold S. Himmelfarb*

These two books are about the contemporary world of Talmud study among Orthodox Jews. Helmreich's book focuses on those who study Talmud as a vocation in post–high school seminaries; Heilman's focuses on those who study it as an avocation in adult study circles in homes, synagogues, and other meeting places.

Because enrollment in a yeshiva beyond high school and participation in an adult study circle are both voluntary activities, Helmreich and Heilman were motivated by a desire to understand the attraction that these groups hold for their participants, beyond the devotion to the sacred imperative of learning Torah. However, the scope of the two studies, their research methodologies, and their disciplinary perspectives, make them very different. Indeed, except for some of the background material on the importance of Torah (particularly Talmudic) study in Jewish culture and the features described above, there is not much that these books have in common.

Helmreich's work on the yeshiva is fairly comprehensive and makes a significant contribution to our understanding of American Orthodoxy today. The growth of these institutions of advanced Torah studies has been mostly a post-World War I phenomenon. Today, according to Helmreich, there are about fifty to sixty yeshivot (plural of yeshiva) in the United States with a combined enrollment of 5,000 students. However, their influence has been much greater than their number implies. Because they educate the rabbinic leadership of Orthodoxy and a significant share of the younger lay leadership, yeshivot have had a tremendous bearing on the resurgence of Orthodoxy in this country and on Orthodoxy's orientation regarding religious and communal matters. Indeed, the traditionalizing of the organized Jewish community at large that has been a consequence of the growing strength of Orthodoxy is undoubtedly rooted in the indirect influence wielded by the yeshivot. Given the relative isolation of a yeshiva environment and the inaccessibility of the uncommitted to its sacred chambers, we must be very grateful for this study that brings the yeshiva into public view.

Helmreich's book is a major contribution not only because it is the first such study but because it is a study of the yeshiva "world" rather than a study of a yeshiva. Its scope, hence, is large. Helmreich presents evidence gathered during six months as a participant observer enrolled in a yeshiva; nearly two hundred interviews with students, faculty, administrators, and key community leaders; a survey of nearly three hundred alumni of one of the largest yeshivot in the United States; and analysis of much written material and many unpublished documents on the subject. He describes the nature of such schools, from the formal organization and curricular content to the informal student-status hierarchy. Helmreich analyzes the isolation of the yeshiva environment, the nature of deviance there and how it is handled, the preparation for life outside the yeshiva (or lack of it), the lasting impact of such education upon its graduates, and the reasons for the growth and survival of the institution. Throughout we are treated to the opinions of the yeshiva students and many of the great contemporary Torah scholars on issues of religious, educational, and societal importance. We read their ideas about Jewish education, relationships with nonobservant Jews, college attendance and career preparation, the rabbinate, dating, marriage, and the role of women. The portrait seems accurate, although many will not be pleased with what they read.

Some readers may be disturbed by Helmreich's uncritical approach. He raises issues and presents the opinions of his respondents on them, but hardly ever takes a personal stand himself. His silence might appear to be acquiescence, yet, one can argue that his method gives the reader the opportunity to form his or her own opinion. Further, the yeshiva world is less likely to close its doors to future researchers if it believes it was negatively evaluated by the first one.

Despite the scope of this study, there is room for much more work in this area. The survey data on the alumni are not analyzed in depth or in a quantitatively sophisticated manner. We get very little information about the parents, except as seen through the eyes of their children. Although it is clear that most of these students are encouraged by their parents to attend a yeshiva, my personal impression is that more than a few parents are made distraught by the continuation of studies for prolonged periods, and the postponment of career preparation or assumption until well into marriage and parenthood. Many households have been upset by what they perceive as extreme observance demanded by the yeshiva of their children, and by their children of them. Parents who considered themselves observant, suddenly find the Orthodoxy of their synagogues, the Kashrut of their homes, their personal behavior regarding sexual modesty, and their relative devotion to sacred matters as opposed to economic matters, all being questioned. Some nonobservant parents believe that their children have been brainwashed in cultlike fashion by these institutions. We could also use research on the yeshiva as a workplace. Helmreich did not study faculty members much, except as they informed him about the students and the curriculum.

Although we look to yeshivot to provide an intellectual leadership for future generations, Helmreich fails to point out that the scholarship engaged in by most of our colleagues in Jewish studies at universities is simply ignored as irrelevant or assumed to be heresy. Thus, the intellectual leadership derived from the yeshivot, although admirable and necessary, must be viewed for what it is within its own limited scope.

The *World of the Yeshiva*, even informed as it is by a sociological perspective, lacks general sociological significance. There is little attempt to relate the phenomena observed to a body of sociological theory, nor is there any attempt to form generalizations beyond the yeshiva itself. Nevertheless, the influence of the yeshiva in American Jewish life makes the book important.

Heilman's *The People of the Book*, in contrast, has important theoretical insights. He examined six Talmud study groups, four of which met in synagogues, one in a home, and one in a social club. One of the groups was observed in the United States; the other five were observed in Jerusalem. The language of instruction was English, Hebrew, or Yiddish, depending on the group.

The chapters outline the basic characteristics of study circles and the *lernen* (learning or studying) activity, which Heilman believes motivates participation in these groups. Basically, he argues that whatever intellectual needs brought people to these study circles, there were also six social functions served that sustained their participation.

The classes had four types of drama, and the students (*lerners*) were swept up in the action. There was *social drama*, during which the relationships among participants and between them and the act of studying were played out. There was *cultural performance*, through which, in the course of talmudic review, the students reacted and rediscovered the meaning of being a Jew. A third form of drama was *interactional drama*, in which "participants played at *lernen* as if it were a game with stylized moves" (p. 25). Fourth, there was drama involved in *word play*, by which members communicated in the special argot of Talmud study and attempted to word things in the proper sequence, intonation, and lyrical rhythm of Talmudic study. Beyond the drama, the groups provided *fellowship and community*. The one group that did not foster fellowship (the one that met at the social club) eventually disbanded. Finally, the groups also helped fulfill a religious obligation. Some people studied Talmud "because they felt a religious obligation to do so. For them *lernen* was a form of worship, an act of homage to their God, nation, history and faith" (p. 25).

Heilman, being an excellent ethnomethodologist, analyzes the subtle forms, gestures, and communications that take place in these classes to illustrate his points. Heilman being an expert storyteller, relates some fascinating tales from his observations to reconstruct for the reader the sense of drama, fellowship, and religious fulfillment that he found in these groups. It is a very well written book, with substantial amounts of theoretical background and anecdotal illustrations.

The points are clear, but I am not sure that they are all that important. Despite the emphasis placed on *lernen* in traditional Judaism, one need not read this book to understand Orthodoxy today. The thesis, however, may be of some importance for educators; particularly those involved in Jewish education at the adolescent and adult levels, where motivation for participation is hard to maintain. Sociologists interested in the phenomena of drama and fellowship in small groups would also find this book of interest. Certainly, some of these phenomena are at work in other types of group activity: card playing, television football watching, some business meetings, and so on. Hence, it is instructive to see how Heilman analyzes them. *The People of the Book* does not offer critical insights into an important aspect of Orthodox Jewish life in the way that Heilman's previous book on the synagogue did. (Perhaps I say this because I am a more involved participant in synagogue "gossip cliques" than in synagogue study circles.)

There is an interesting contrast betweeen the two books reviewed here as contributions to the sociology of Jewry. Helmreich's book lacks theoretical insight and generalization, but is significant because it is a fairly comprehensive study of an important aspect of Jewish life. Heilman's study is filled with theoretical insights and generalizations, but the phenomenon studied is rather trivial for our broader understanding of Jewish or Orthodox life in contemporary times. There are so few of us working actively in this field that we should all assume the obligation of trying to fulfill both mandates: to study significant phenomena and to contribute to the theoretical understanding of Jewish life and human behavior generally.

11

American Jewry: Survival or Revival?

American Modernity and Jewish Identity
by Steven M. Cohen.
New York: Methuen, 1983. 250 pp. $22.00 cloth. $8.95 paper.

American Jews in Transition
by Chaim Waxman.
Philadelphia: Temple Univesity Press, 1983. 290 pp. $24.95 cloth. $9.95
paper.

Reviewed by *Carol Poll*

A sociological analysis of American Jewry is the subject of these two
books. Both books go beyond the usual discussion of assimilation and
present us with analytical descriptions of the development and current
state of Jewish life in the United States.

Steven Cohen's book can be seen as two books in one. In the first part of
his book he delineates his "modernization perspective," in which he draws
"instructive parallels" from the responses of past Jewish communities in
Europe to modernization and the present situation in this country. In the
second part of his book, chapters 3 through 8, he analyzes generational
change in religious practices and Jewish identification based primarily on
an analysis of surveys of Boston Jews in 1965 ($N = 1,569$) and 1975
($N = 934$) viewed through the lens of his modernization perspective. Cohen concludes that the Jewish response to modernity was a reformulation
of religious practices and beliefs to comport with the demands of modern
thinking. "The vast majority of Western Jews . . . to integrate into the social
mainstream sharply reduced the scope and intensity of their subcultural
involvement. Second, so as to survive as Jews, they innovated new modes
of Jewish identity and community." Thus, according to Cohen, first-gener-
ation Jews tended to be Orthodox, and third- and fourth-generation Jews

are primarily Reform in denominational preference as a consequence of their attempts to modernize.

Cohen devotes five chapters to analyzing carefully the survey data in terms of how they shed light on such issues as the impact on Jewish identification, group integration, ethnic survival of social status, residential mobility and community, liberalism, pro-Israelism, and alternative families that include female-headed households, singles, and intermarrieds.

Among the conclusions Cohen draws from this analysis is that a growing number of alternative households probably poses the greatest challenge to Jewish continuity of all the demographic consequences of modern integration. He also concludes that the advancement of each generation brought the erosion of certain traditional ritual practices and stabilization in the practice of more modern observances (e.g., the dietary laws are generally ignored, but Passover is generally observed as a family get-together).

Cohen's book provides many interesting data and raises many questions. Survey data, as Cohen himself points out, have serious limitations. Responses to focused questions on a questionnaire, do not, I believe, provide us with enough information to get a full picture of the subtleties of religious practice, behavior, and identification. For example, Cohen tells us that in his 1975 sample, 18 percent of the young singles report that they light Sabbath candles, but only 12 percent report that they attend services and 16 percent report that they are synagogue members. One wonders, who are these "closet" Sabbath candle lighters? Are they women, men, Orthodox, Conservative, Reform, Havurah, or unaffiliated Jews? What does candle lighting mean to them? One would welcome a follow-up book by Cohen presenting us with data based on in-depth interviews and participant observational data concerning the many interesting points with which he deals.

In *American Jews in Transition* Chaim Waxman tells the story of the American Jewish experience, skillfully recounting social history while engaging in sociological analysis. He accomplishes the rare sociological feat of synthesizing quantitative and qualitative studies as well as primary and secondary historical data to form a book that is as captivating as a well-written novel.

Waxman begins by describing the nature of the Jewish community in its formative years, 1654-1880. He details the social systems of the first and second waves of immigration, those of the Sephardic and German Jews, and the responses of the larger society to them. He then proceeds to the heart of the story, the immigration of the Eastern European Jews who swelled the ranks of American Jewry from 250,000 in 1880 to 3.5 million in 1917. It was this group that formed the first generation of most of the Jews in the United States today. They were "Orthoprax," that is, they were not ideologically committed to Orthodox beliefs but continued to adhere to Orthodox practice just as they had done when they lived in the shtetl. In Europe most Jews had "shared a common religion, language, set of values, norms, institutional structures, a sense of belonging . . . and were perceived by themselves and non-Jews as a separate nation." It was this group experience that gave American Jews their religioethnic self-perception.

The second generation was the ones who moved in the 1920s and 1930s from the Lower East Sides to the Bronxes and Brooklyns of the nation. They tried to melt into the giant melting pot but instead faced quotas limiting college entrance and excluding them from certain jobs and clubs. The second generation embraced Conservative Judaism, which it perceived as a progressive form of Judaism and which, at the same time, was rooted in tradition.

The third generation, that of the fifties and sixties, was solidly middle-class suburbanites who, unlike their non-Jewish neighbors, voted for and espoused politically liberal causes. This third generation was "religious without religiosity," defining itself as a religious group and not as an ethnic group, thus using religion for social identification purposes although most traditional religious rituals were eliminated. It was this group and its children that numerous sociological studies foresaw as headed for assimilation.

Waxman suggests that in the fourth generation, the 1970s and 1980s, the pendulum has swung and, instead of assimilation, what appears to be occurring is a renaissance of Judaism. He identifies several factors contributing to this phenomenon, including (1) the growth of a young professional modern Orthodox group that is both ideologically and behaviorally committed to Orthodoxy as a result of having been educated in the yeshivot begun by the Orthodox rabbinical community that emigrated to the United States after World War II; (2) the development of a survivalist mentality among American Jews as a result of the 1967 Six Day War that forced them to confront the possibility of another Holocaust whereby Israel could be destroyed while the world stood by and watched; and (3) the develoment of a Black separatist movement that legitimated ethnic pride and cultural pluralism.

Waxman's later chapters deal with other aspects of the contemporary American Jewish community, including occupational patterns, political behavior, geographic patterns, income patterns, political attitudes and behavior, denominational patterns, Jewish education, decision making, and patterns of anti-Semitism, with an insightful analysis of the issues surrounding Black anti-Semitism. He devotes a complete chapter to a discussion of the contemporary American Jewish family that attempts to synthesize the various studies on this topic. However, this reader feels that many more qualitative studies, including in-depth interviews with Jewish families, are needed to flesh out the picture and determine if there is a distinctive life-style in the fourth-generation Jewish family. Are there distinctively Jewish child-rearing patterns, sex-role divisions of labor, patterns of communication, role performance and expectations, and other family dynamics?

One of the factors that make Waxman's book stand out is his unabashedly survivalist perspective. He rejects what he calls the "simplistic notions of so-called value-free sociology." He shows how previous studies, many of which predicted the assimilation of Jews in the United States, were incorrect because they were based on the faulty notion that Jews were merely an ethnic group, when, in fact, they are a religioethnic group. Unlike Cohen, who emphasizes theory and survey data, Waxman weaves a keen sense of the sacred and transcendental into his secular analysis to create a vibrant picture of Jewish life in the United States.

12

Crisis in American Jewry

A Certain People: American Jews and Their Lives Today
by Charles E. Silberman.
New York: Summit Books, 1985. 458 pp. $19.95.

Reviewed by *Steven Bayme*

Charles Silberman's long-awaited work on American Jewry synthesizes
the most recent sociological research and demographic studies into a co-
herent and thoughtful analysis of the state of American Jewry. The book's
dustjacket identifies Silberman as the well-known author of *Crisis in Black
and White* and *Crisis in the Classroom*. Would we now be treated to a
"Crisis in American Jewry"?

Silberman answers this question in resoundingly negative terms. Neither
external foes nor internal erosion threaten American Jewish continuity.
On the contrary, Silberman celebrates the major changes in American
society that have opened virtually all portals to Jews. Formerly closed or
restricted aspects of the power structure now willingly accept Jews into
their highest echelons. Since World War II anti-Semitism has been in general retreat. Even the much-publicized AWACs debate five years ago is
today largely forgotten. Only among young and well-educated Blacks does
Silberman perceive significant signs of anti-Semitism.

Nor, in Silberman's view, ought Jews agonize over low fertility and high
intermarriage rates. Jews remain overwhelmingly committed to marriage
and a norm of two children—small, but enough to replace themselves, and
Jewish familes were never large in any case. Although intermarriage has
risen to 25 percent, this rate is far lower than the usual estimates paraded
for U.S. audiences. Moreover, in light of the increasing tendency of intermarrieds to raise their children as Jews, intermarriage may result in a net
gain for the Jewish community. Finally, the open U.S. society has given
Jews the freedom to choose to lead a Jewish life. When the mountain of

tradition no longer hangs over them, as in the midrashic rendition of God compelling the Jews to accept the Torah, those who freely choose to lead a Jewish life do so with vigor and intensity.

Yet, if the news is so good, why has the book received a fairly harsh press? No doubt many Jews have a natural paranoia about their future. One generation after the Holocaust, we have witnessed the enormous capacities of anti-Semitism. The phenomenom has existed, at least in latent form, in every society in which Jews have sought to preserve a corporate identity as Jews. Only the factors that trigger anti-Semitism and transform it into a real danger for Jews have varied. In that light, it is at least questionable whether the United States is really different from other societies in which Jews have prospered.

In terms of the United States, however, every survey taken since World War II has reported a decline in anti-Semitic attitudes. Even during difficult times, e.g., the Lebanon War, public support for Israel and regard for Jews remained high. American Jews suffer no important disabilities. Jews have at times been considered for the vice-presidency of the country. Critical phenomena—McCarthyism, the George Wallace presidential campaign, the oil boycott—were noticeably free of anti-Semitic content, although at another place and time such currents usually were accompanied by widespread agitation against Jews. To be sure, anti-Semitism among Blacks did flare during the controversy over Andrew Young's resignation and more recently during Jesse Jackson's presidential bid. Clearly, Jews may not relax their guard, but by historical standards their situation in the United States is most enviable.

Still, Silberman's optimism rings hollow with respect to the internal condition of Jewry. First, Silberman celebrates Jewish affluence and general professional success. Estimates of Jewish poverty, however, remain around 10 percent. One of four Jewish wage earners do not attend college and in all likelihood enter blue-collar occupations. Inner-city Jews, frequently residing in high-crime neighborhoods without close family, pass unnoticed in Silberman's book. Irving Shapiro of DuPont no more typifies the American Jew than does an elderly shut-in in New York's Lower East Side.

Nor does Silberman manage to persuade that the news is good on fertility and intermarriage. He argues that Jews are delaying childbearing into their thirties but still expect two or more children. Yet Silberman fails to account for the increase in infertility among women over age thirty. Nor does he question whether long-term involvement in careers may inhibit childbearing even if biological capacity and desire exist. Finally, he does not examine how Jewish tradition will be transmitted in the two-career family. Current fertility trends herald both quantitative and qualitative changes in the Jewish population.

In terms of intermarriage Silberman badly underestimates the dangers intermarriage poses both to Jewish continuity and to communal unity. The logic of his argument that intermarriage will mean a net gain of Jews should lead one to advocate increased intermarriage. More tellingly, if no conversion occurs, it is most questionable whether substantive Jewish content will continue to be transmitted. Children of intermarrieds are unlikely to seek out Jewish mates if they see their parents as successfully intermarried. Impressionistic evidence—at least as persuasive as Silberman's "Items"—points to large numbers of intermarrieds raising their children within a dual-faith framework. One would have to redefine Judaism radically to continue to count these as Jews or to place much hope in the Jewishness of their children. To be sure, evidence does exist that Jews by choice act like most other Jews and frequently enhance the community. Yet, in the absence of conversion, the residue of Jewish identity carried by the Jewish spouse is unlikely to be transmitted to the next generation. Finally, although Silberman downplays the rates of intermarriage, they are clearly high by historical standards. Most tellingly, he cites a 1975 Boston survey to the effect that only 16 percent of Jews aged eighteen to twenty-nine would oppose intermarriage. If Jews are at best neutral on the subject, while the heads of the religious movements unanimously oppose intermarriage, we do have a crisis of norms and values.

Moreover, Silberman fails to gauge how differing attitudes toward intermarriage and conversion threaten to undermine communal unity. He rightly criticizes the Orthodox for their unwillingness to consider possible models of a unified conversion procedure acceptable to all the religious movements, yet fails to acknowledge that the decision by the Reform and Reconstructionist movements to define the child of a Jewish father and a non-Jewish mother as a Jew heralds a crisis over who is a Jew. The decision informs intermarried couples in which the male is Jewish that their children are Jewish. Yet Conservative and Orthodox Jews agree that such a definition is unacceptable, and they will not accept such individuals as Jews. Silberman casually predicts that Conservative Judaism will soon adopt patrilineality, presumably on the grounds that several Conservative rabbis favor it. For the present, however, the Rabbinical Assembly has overwhelmingly rejected patrilineality as does the incoming chancellor of the Jewish Theological Seminary. A schism in the community seems just around the corner.

Finally, Silberman has little to say about Jewish education. Jewish day schools are thriving, but strangely Silberman chooses to ignore them. Supplementary schools, which continue to attract the bulk of Jewish students, suffer from insufficient contact hours, shortage of qualified personnel, and an overwhelming dropout rate after bar or bat mitzvah. Silberman seems content to observe that about 50 percent of Jewish children receive some Jewish education, without commenting on its quality. Yet clearly, in the open society the least-educated Jews are the most likely to opt to join the larger community. In that sense, the sorry state of Jewish education does herald a "crisis in American Jewry."

To be sure, there are signs of Jewish renewal. Many adults are discovering their Jewish identity for the first time. American Jews have become less self-conscious about their Jewishness and more willing to identify publicly as Jews. Yet we must question the depth and intensity of the renewal when Jews no longer reject intermarriage and are unversed in the traditions, culture, and values—to say nothing of the language—of their people.

Charles Silberman's important new book serves as an excellent introduction to the inner and outer lives of American Jews. One may agree with his basic theme of Jewish renewal and be optimistic about the prospects for Jewish continuity into the next century. Let us acknowledge, however, the serious dangers that Jews confront in terms of Jewish family, literacy, and communal unity.

APPENDIX

Recent Research on Contemporary Jewry: A Compendium of Citations of Abstracts

Rena Cheskis-Gold and *Arnold Dashefsky*

Continuing a pattern established in Volume 7, *Contemporary Jewry* presents citations of abstracts of journal articles on the sociological study of Jewry. An initial computer search for 1983 and 1984 provided by Sociological Abstracts yielded a list of titles and authors that was developed from the following root words: holocaust, Israel, Jew, Jud (aic/aism), and synagogue. We then eliminated articles in the following categories: (1) those that were only marginally social scientific (mainly technical sociolinguistic pieces), (2) those dealing with Palestinians with no reference to Jewish or Israeli society, (3) historical articles about Jewish individuals that were not placed in the context of Jewish communities or society, (4) research studies conducted in Israel that could have as easily been set in other countries because no reference was made to uniquely Jewish/Israeli issues (e.g. ideology, ethnicity, immigration, unique government policy laws). The results yielded a total of 72 citations, 17 for 1983 and 55 for 1984. Each entry is presented with the accession number for reference, which is then followed by the author (s) and the title. The reader may then consult *Sociological Abstracts* for the complete abstract.

The articles are listed in alphabetical order according to the following subfields or categories:

Adolescence and Youth
American Sociological Association
Association for Women in Development
Bureaucratic Structures
Delinquency
Demography
Feminist Studies
Group Interactions
Industrial Sociology (Labor)
Institut International de Sociologie
International Sociological Association/Sociology of
    Education Research Section

Military Sociology
North Central Sociological Association
Personality and Culture
Political Sociology
Research Technology
Rural Sociology (Village, Agriculture)
Rural Sociological Society
Social Differentiation
Social Disorganization (Crime)
Social Stratification/Mobility
Society for the Study of Social Problems
Sociology of Education
Sociology of the Family
Sociology of Language and Literature
Sociology of Leisure
Sociology of Religion
Sociology of Science
Sociology of Social Behavior
Studies in Violence

We welcome comments from readers on the usefulness of this compendium of citations of abstracts. In particular, we would like to hear readers'
ideas about additional fields or subfields of the literature that they might
like to see included, especially in light of the fact that discussions are
ongoing to publish a professional journal of complete abstracts in the
social scientific study of Jewry.

Adolescence and Youth

8401832.   Florian, Victor, The Impact of Social Environment and Sex
on Adolescent Social Values: A Comparison of the Kibbutz
and the City in Israel.

American Sociological Association

83S15773.   Dashefsky, Arnold, DeAmicis, Jan & Lazerwitz, Bernard,
American Emigration: Similarities and Differences among
Migrants to Australia and Israel.

84S16512.   Johnston, Barry V., Columbus Country: The Russian Slav
and Jew in the United States.

84S16589. Semyonov, Moshe, Sport and Beyond: Ethnic Inequalities in Attainment.

Association for Women in Development

84S16623. Taplin, Ruth, The Position of Women in the Israeli Kibbutz System: Linkages and Effects.

Bureaucratic Structures

84N9434. Karabel, Jerome, Status-Group Struggle, Organizational Interests, and the Limits of Institutional Autonomy: The Transformation of Harvard, Yale, and Princeton, 1918-1940.

Delinquency

8400387. Hassin, Yael, Juvenile Delinquency in Israel, 1948-1977: Patterns and Trends.

Demography & Human Biology

84N8336. Basker, Eileen, Coping with Fertility in Israel: A Case Study of Culture Clash.

8401746. Berman, Yitzhak & Eaglstein, A. Solomon, Social Factors as Predictors of Internal Migration Patterns in Israel.

8403675. Berman, Yitzhak, Immigration to Israel: Ideology vs. Reality.

Family and Socialization

84N8416. Shurka, Esther & Florian, Victor, A Study of Israeli Jewish and Arab Parental Perceptions of Their Disabled Children.

84N8421. Weil, Shalva, The Effect of Ethnic Origin on Children's Perceptions of Their Families.

Feminist Studies

84N6969. Bernstein, Deborah, The Plough Woman Who Cried into the Pots: The Position of Women in the Labor Force in the Pre-State Israeli Society.

8402215.   Hartman, Harriet & Hartman, Moshe, The Effect of Immigration on Women's Roles in Various Countries.

Group Interactions

84N7500.   Kirschenbaum, Alan, Segregated Integration: A Research Note on the Fallacy of Misplaced Numbers.

84N7524.   Smith, Tom W. & Dempsey, Glenn R., The Polls: Ethnic Social Distance and Prejudice.

84N7526.   Smooha, Sammy, Minority Responses in a Plural Society: A Typology of the Arabs in Israel.

84N9313.   Seligson, Mitchell A. & Caspi, Dan, Arabs in Israel: Political Tolerance and Ethnic Conflict.

8402748.   Cohn, Werner, The Name Changers.

8402759.   Himmelfarb, Harold S. & Loar, R. Michael, National Trends in Jewish Ethnicity: A Test of the Polarization Hypothesis.

8402783.   Schoenfeld, Stuart, The Transmission of Jewish Identity among Families in a Non-Jewish Neighborhood.

8402788.   Silbermann, Alphons, Research in Prejudice and Historiography.

8402792.   Swirski, Shlomo, The Oriental Jews in Israel: Why Many Tilted toward Begin.

8402793.   Tsukashima, Ronald Tadao, Chronological, Cognitive, and Political Effects in the Study of Inter-Minority Group Prejudice.

8402800.   Weinfeld, Morton, The Ethnic Sub-Economy: Explication and Analysis of a Case Study of the Jews of Montreal.

Industrial Sociology
(Labor)

84N5887.   Mannheim, Bilha, Male and Female Industrial Workers: Job Satisfaction, Work Role Centrality, and Work Place Preference.

Institut International de Sociologie

84S16630. Taplin, Ruth, The Chinese Commune and Israeli Kibbutz: Comparative Analysis.

International Sociological Association
Sociology of Education Research Section

84S16190. Yogev, Abraham & Chen, Michael, Sponsorship as School Charter: Educational Mobility in Religious versus Secular Schools in Israel.

Military Sociology

83N2748. Naveh, David, Inter-Bureaucratic Civil-Military Relations in Israel: The Case of Planning Post-Peace Military Redeployment.

North Central Sociological Association

83S15906. Wolf, Allan B., Responding to Transition: A Study of the Taylor Rd. Jewish Community.

83S15304. Mork, Gordon R., Assimilation and Nationalism among Nineteenth-Century German Jews: An Historian's Questions to the Sociologists.

84S16040. Matre, Marc, Identity, Belief, and Involvement in a Small Jewish Community.

Personality and Culture

83N2447. Jacobsen, Chanoch, Differences in Normative Expectations and Their Implications.

83N4040. Bar Yosef, Rivka W. & Lieblich, Anna, Comments on Brandow's "Ideology, Myth, and Reality: Sex Equality in Israel."

8400938. Tec, Nechama, Righteous Christians in Poland.

8402602. Aboud, Francis B. & Skerry, Shelagh A., Self and Ethnic Concepts in Relation to Ethnic Constancy.

8402635.   Florian, Victor & Har-Even, Dov, Fear of Personal Death: The Effects of Sex and Religious Belief.

8402717.   Verbit, Mervin E., Jewish Identity and the Israel-Diaspora Dialogue.

Political Sociology

83N4446.   Chafetz, Janet Saltzman & Ebaugh, Helen Rose Fuchs, Growing Conservatism in the United States? An Examination of Trends in Political Opinion between 1972 and 1980.

84N6077.   Kaufman, Menahem, A Trust Betrayed: The American Trusteeship Proposal for Palestine in 1948.

Research Technology

83N3787.   Himmelfarb, Harold, Loar, R. Michael & Mott, Susan, Sampling by Ethnic Surnames: The Case of American Jews.

Rural Sociology
(Village, Agriculture)

84N6222.   Avni, Haim, Jewish Agriculture in Argentina: Success or Failure?

Rural Sociological Society

83S15451.   Shapiro, Ovadia, Rural Sociology and Rural Development in Israel.

Social Change & Economic Development

8401170.   Bernstein, Deborah, Economic Growth and Female Labour: The Case of Israel.

Social Differentiation

83N2930.   Adler, Israel & Hodge, Robert W., Ethnicity and the Process of Status Attainment in Israel.

Social Disorganization
(Crime)

8400373.   Sebba, Leslie, Attitudes of New Immigrants toward White-Collar Crime: A Cross-Cultural Exploration.

Social Stratification/Mobility

84N9651.   Cohen, Percy S., Ethnicity, Class, and Political Alignment in Israel.

84N9676.   Semyonov, Moshe & Kraus, Vered, Gender, Ethnicity and Income Inequality: The Israeli Experience.

Society for the Study of Social Problems

83S15635.   Tabory, Ephraim, Religious Inter-Relationships in an Israeli Community.

84S16413.   Young, Allen H. & Taplin, Ruth, The Impact of Socialist Industrialization on the Community: A Comparative Study of the Chinese Commune and Israeli Kibbutz.

Sociology of Education

84N6383.   Shaffir, William, The Recruitment of Baalei Tshuvah in a Jerusalem Yeshiva.

84N9881.   Shavit, Yossi, Tracking and Ethnicity in Israeli Secondary Education.

Sociology of the Family

83N3397.   Davids, Leo, What's Happening in the Israeli Family? Recent Demographic Trends.

84N6640.   Cherlin, Andrew & Celebuski, Carin, Are Jewish Families Different? Some Evidence from the General Social Survey.

84N6713.   Yogev, Abraham & Jamshy, Haia, Children of Ethnic Intermarriage in Israeli Schools: Are They Marginal?

8400250.   Winkler, Iris & Doherty, William, J., Communication Styles and Marital Satisfaction in Israeli and American Couples.

8403749.   Ben-Rafael, Eliezer & Weitman, Sasha, The Reconstitution of the Family in the Kibbutz.

Sociology of Language and Literature

84N6339.   Rosenbaum, Yehudit, Hebrew Adoption among New Immigrants to Israel: The First Three Years.

84N6344.   Weil, Shalva, Woman and Language in Israel.

Sociology of Leisure

84N6026.   Shamir, Boas & Ruskin, Hillel, Type of Community as a Moderator of Work-Leisure Relationships: A Comparative Study of Kibbutz Residents and Urban Residents.

Sociology of Religion

83N1512.   Liebman, Charles S., Extremism as a Religious Norm.

83N3148.   Tabory, Ephraim & Lazerwitz, Bernard, Americans in the Israeli Reform and Conservative Denominations: Religiosity under an Ethnic Shield.

83N3153.   Weissbrod, Lilly, Religion as National Identity in a Secular Society.

83N4797.   Fishman, Aryei, Judaism and Modernization: The Case of the Religious Kibbutzim.

84N8199.   Dashefsky, Arnold & Lazerwitz, Bernard, The Role of Religious Identification in North American Migration to Israel.

84N8209.   Hartman, Moshe, Pronatalistic Tendencies and Religiosity in Israel.

84N9941.   Shaffir, William, Hassidic Jews and Quebec Politics.

84N9943.   Silbermann, Alphons, Aspects of Public Transmission of the History of Judaism.

Sociology of Science

83N3238.   Toren, Nina & Griffel, Avi, A Cross-Cultural Examination of Scientists' Perceived Importance of Work Characteristics.

84N8331.   Toren, Nina, Attitudes towards Work: A Comparison of Soviet and American Immigrant Scientists in Israel.

Sociology of Sexual Behavior

8400200.   Notzer, Netta, Levran, David, Mashiach, Shlomo & Soffer, Sarah, Effects of Religiosity on Sex Attitudes, Experience and Contraception among University Students.

Studies in Violence

8402181.   Diner, Dan, Israel and the Trauma of the Mass Extermination.

About the Contributors

Steven Bayme is the Assistant National Director of the American Jewish Committee's Jewish Communal Affairs Department, which is generally concerned with Jewish continuity and the inner vitality of American Jews.

Jay Y. Brodbar-Nemzer is currently a Jerusalem Fellow studying issues in Jewish education. His research interests center on the Jewish family, including divorce, marital relationships, intermarriage attitudes, and the transmission of Jewish identity.

Rena Cheskis-Gold works as a demographer for Yale University's Office of Institutional Research. Her current research is diverse, ranging from a study of intermarriage and conversion among Catholics to an economic model of student loan default.

Arnold Dashefsky is Associate Professor of Sociology and Direcctor of the Center for Judaic Studies and Contemporary Jewish Life at the University of Connecticut. His current research interests focus on a comparative investigation of the sources and consequences of American emigration (to Australia and Israel, with J. DeAmicis and B. Lazerwitz) and an analysis of the determinants of Jewish charitable giving.

Calvin Goldscheider is Professor of Judaic Studies and Sociology at Brown University and associated with its Population Studies and Training Center. His research in Judaic Studies focuses on the comparative-historical analysis of contemporary Jewries, including the sociological analysis of American, Israeli, and European Jewish communities.

Harold S. Himmelfarb is Associate Professor in the Department of Sociology at the Ohio State University. He is immediate past President of the ASSJ and has just completed editing (with Sergio DellaPergolla) *Jewish Education Worldwide: Cross Cultural Perspectives*, to be released in late 1986.

Vivian Klaff is Associate Professor in the Department of Sociology at the University of Delaware. His current research interests are the analysis of the urban ecology of the Jews in the Diaspora, development of microcomputer software for teaching demography, and the impact of school desegregation programs on racial residential segregation in U.S. cities.

Samuel Z. Klausner is Professor of Sociology at the University of Pennsylvania and Director of the Center for Research on the Acts of Man. He offers a course in the sociology of Jewry as part of Penn's Judaic Studies Program and is currently analyzing data on the mobility of Jews in the United States corporate world.

Bernard Lazerwitz is Professor of Sociology at Bar-Ilan University in Israel. Currently, he is directing a survey of Tel Aviv that has a variety of goals; among them is that of contrasting Israeli and American Jewish community involvement and Jewish self-images.

Carol Poll is a member of the adjunct faculty of the Fashion Institute of Technology of the State University of New York, an Educator in Special Education for the New York City Board of Education, and a *rebbitzen*. Her research interests include gender roles in Judaism, the sociology of educational equity, and special education.

J. Alan Winter is currently Professor of Sociology at Connecticut College. He is the author of *Continuities in the Sociology of Religion*. His most recent work is a study of the cost of living Jewishly, conducted under the auspices of the Council of Jewish Federation, for which he recently served as a research consultant.

Jonathan S. Woocher is Executive Vice-President of Jewish Education Services of North America. He has taught at Brandeis University and conducts research on American Jewish communal organization and ideology.

Alan York is a lecturer in the School of Social Work, Bar-Ilan University, Ramat-Gan, Israel. His major research interests are in the sociological fields of voluntarism and voluntary associations and in the practice and theory of community social work.

Walter P. Zenner is Associate Professor of Anthropology at S.U.N.Y.-Albany and is editor of the Anthropology and Judaic Studies for SUNY Press. His research interests include middleman minorities and Sephardic Jews in the United States and Israel.